Quilting
Handbook

Quilting
Handbook

THUNDER BAY
P · R · E · S · S

San Diego, California

Thunder Bay Press
An imprint of the Advantage Publishers Group
THUNDER BAY 5880 Oberlin Drive, San Diego, CA 92121-4794
P·R·E·S·S www.thunderbaybooks.com

Library of Congress Cataloging-in-Publication Data

Quilting handbook.
   p. cm.
  ISBN 1-59223-174-8
   1. Patchwork-Patterns. 2. Quilting-Patterns.

 TT835.Q5444 2003
 746.46'041--dc22

                                                     2003061609

QUMQDZZ

Manufactured in Singapore by Pica Digital Pte Ltd
Printed in China by CT Printing Ltd.

1 2 3 4 5 08 07 06 05 04

CONTENTS

INTRODUCTION 7

EQUIPMENT & MATERIALS 11

TECHNIQUES 25
    stitches 26
    traditional quilting 34
    contour quilting 38
    shadow quilting 42
    random quilting 46
    tied quilting 50
    trapunto quilting 54
    corded quilting 57
    sashiko quilting 60
    quilting and appliqué 63
    quilting and patchwork 67

PROJECTS 73
    1 & 2 using traditional quilting 74
    3 using contour quilting 82
    4 & 5 using shadow quilting 87
    6 & 7 using random quilting 97
    8 & 9 using tied quilting 108
    10 & 11 using trapunto quilting 117
    12 using corded quilting 128
    13 using sashiko quilting 136
    14–17 using quilting and appliqué 141
    18–22 using quilting and patchwork 164

INSPIRATION FROM FINE ARTISTS 191

DESIGNING YOUR OWN QUILT 205

PATTERNS 209

GLOSSARY 220

INDEX 222

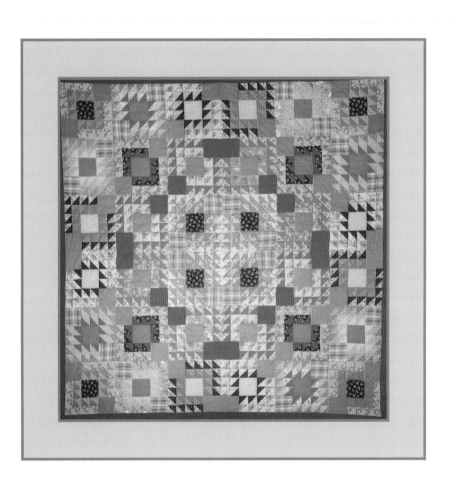

INTRODUCTION

In recent years there has been an astonishing growth of interest in all fabric crafts, but none so enthusiastically sustained as in quilting, patchwork, and appliqué. For many people, the terms "quilting" and "patchwork" are synonymous with patchwork quilt, and although they are traditionally combined in certain types of quilt-making, each technique is a needlecraft in its own right – since there are many bedcovers made in patchwork that are not quilted, as well as those that are quilted but not patched or appliquéd. However, on a domestic level, the "evolution" of all three needlecrafts is very closely linked with the development of the quilt.

Although bedcovers made by quilting, patchwork, and appliqué have been made by rich and poor alike all over the world, from China to Peru, and have been a vital form of creative expression for countless women over the past 300 years, their individual beginnings go back to ancient history. Unfortunately, owing to the perishable nature of textiles, few original examples have survived, but various references are made in both early writings and on ancient architectural frescoes and carvings. Possibly the oldest recorded example of quilting is a Siberian carpet estimated to have been made during the first century BC. This was discovered on the floor of a tomb during the Koslov expedition in 1924–25 and is now in the Leningrad

Department of Archaeology of the Academy of Sciences. The earliest known example of patchwork is a votive hanging that was found in the Cave of the Thousand Buddhas in India and dates from the sixth century — although records show that both patchwork and appliqué were used in ancient Greece and in Egypt as early as 1000 BC. It is also known that traders from ancient China sold mosaic patchwork made from silk and brocade, and that in India, tents were highly decorated with hangings and friezes of appliqué and quilted designs. Turkish foot soldiers wore quilted garments under their armor for warmth and to prevent chafing, as did the Chinese.

Like other traditional needlecrafts, their exact origins are not known, but all three techniques are thought to have begun in the East (where weaving and trading in woven fabrics began) and then traveled via the Oriental trade routes to Asia, Europe, and the West. It must have taken about 2,000 years for these needlecrafts to reach Britain, during which time various adaptations were made — changes related to domestic economy and local prevailing climatic conditions — and so there developed the individual styles that we know today. To survive the severely cold winters of northern countries, for example, warm garments, carpets, and bedcovers were made with thick interlinings of sheep's wool or rags, which later came to be known as wadded quilting. To eke out sufficient fabric for the top layers — which would be homespun and relatively scarce — odds and ends and even the good parts of old garments would be salvaged and pieced together, thus making a simple type of patchwork. In more temperate climates thinner interlinings and lighter forms of quilting evolved, notably corded and padded (Italian and trapunto). Here very fine silk and linen ground fabrics were used, and often combined surface embroidery and pulled threadwork, so that the finished effect became more and more decorative. Two of the earliest surviving pieces of trapunto quilting are a pair of Sicilian quilts, dated 1395, that are beautifully worked on natural linen with brown thread. In each case, the entire surface is divided into rectangular shapes, filled with complex pictorial scenes depicting figures, animals, and lettering from the legendary story of Tristram.

Skills are believed to have been introduced into Britain by the

Crusaders on their return from Europe during the twelfth and thirteenth centuries. Eventually, quilting frames were devised and the art of quilt-making in Britain flourished. Allover designs were found to be more durable than earlier random stitching, and all kinds of scroll-like patterns and pictorial designs became popular. Quilting, patchwork, and appliqué were combined in many forms, and needlework in general became more complicated. Appliqué was used to display colorful heraldic devices on standards and colors, heralds' tabards, surcoats, and flags, and on ecclesiastical banners and vestments. Symbolic motifs cut from rich velvets, silks, and damasks were applied to equally sumptuous ground fabrics and lavishly embroidered with silk, pure gold, and silver threads.

From the time of the Middle Ages, appliqué in Europe was a highly sophisticated craft worked by professional embroiderers specializing in ecclesiastical, heraldic, and all other official and civic regalia—as it still is today.

By the late sixteenth century quilting in England was a firmly established trade. It continued through the 1700s when fashionable garments, such as waistcoats, petticoats, and hats, were decoratively quilted for the wealthy, as were complete sets of bed furnishings.

During the 1700s, settlers moving out to the New World had taken these skills to America. With limited supplies of fabric, patchwork was used as a quick and thrifty means to making much-needed bedcovers—and thus began the great American patchwork tradition. In order to speed up piecing, the block and set were devised whereby plain strips of fabric were set between pieced blocks. This provided a new design element and a grid on which hundreds of patchwork patterns have since been based.

In more recent times, machine-made blankets, central heating, and the duvet have all contributed to the decline of homemade quilt-making—but the innate desire to create remains. Apart from the current spontaneous revival in quilt-making, much energy has been rechanneled into contemporary quilting, patchwork, and appliqué, evolving over the years into new and exciting art forms. Where the general approach is more experimental and self-expressive, individual designers have excelled. These works have given the fabric crafts a value and an entirely new status—and in some instances should be judged as pieces of fine art.

EQUIPMENT & MATERIALS

The basic equipment needed for quilting, patchwork, and appliqué is not elaborate and can be bought at most department stores or needlework and art suppliers. When you begin to gather your tools and equipment together, you will probably find that you already have several items in your toolbox or around the home.

The idea of making something both beautiful and useful from materials that may be discarded or which cost little is very appealing, especially in today's climate of conservation and recycling.

There are many fabric stores that supply materials and equipment specifically for the quilt-maker, and the range of colors and prints available is almost unlimited. Most of the necessary equipment is the same as that for dressmaking, with one or two additions.

General Drawing Equipment

For designing, marking fabrics, and making templates, you will need rulers (both plastic and metal), a set square (right-angle triangle), a protractor, a pair of compasses, and a range of colored crayons, lead pencils, and chalk pencils — a set of felt pens is also useful for making your own designs. There are various proprietary "magic" markers available for transferring designs to fabric. These are particularly useful for quilting, where it is crucial to have a lightly marked design that does not permanently mark the fabric. You will also need a sharp knife.

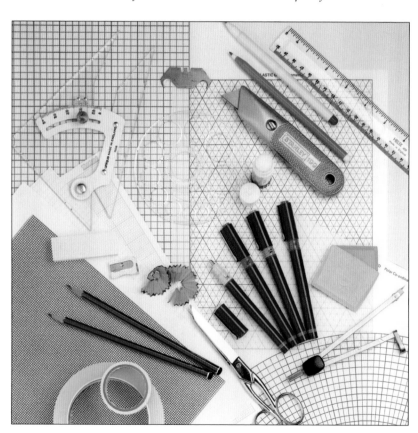

EQUIPMENT FOR DESIGNING AND ENLARGING PATTERNS

Standard pencils, erasers, rulers, and drawing paper are used for drawing and tracing designs, but dressmaker's or ordinary graph paper is useful when enlarging them.

Quilting designs are often available as stencils, but if you want to make your own stencils, template plastic is ideal. Some stores also sell special graph boards or shaped templates (circles, diamonds, or triangles) marked with different divisions, which save a great deal of measuring and drawing when you are designing your own quilting or patchwork patterns.

It's often important to draw up quilting and patchwork designs very accurately. As shown on the opposite page, supplement ordinary drawing equipment with specialized graph paper and template plastic.

EQUIPMENT FOR TRANSFERRING PATTERNS

There are many different ways of transferring patterns to your fabric, and the method will vary according to the pattern, the fabric, and whether or not the traced lines will be covered by the stitching.

On pale fabrics, patterns can often be traced, either in soft pencil, if the lines will be covered, or using a special water-soluble or fading pen. You can do this by laying the fabric over the design, which you have drawn over with black pen so it shows through the fabric, and tracing over the lines you can see. Or you can tape the design and fabric to a window and trace the lines of the design beneath (the advantage of this latter method is that even fine lines are clearly visible as the light shines through the paper and fabric).

Water-soluble pen marks can be sponged away with a damp cloth when the stitching is complete, while fading pen marks gradually disappear — often within twenty-four hours, so don't mark a large area in this way!

On dark fabrics you can use tailor's chalk. Dressmaker's carbon paper is available in various colors and is used in the same way as ordinary carbon paper. You lay the paper, carbon side down, on the right side of the fabric, then cover it with the paper holding your design and trace over the design with a pencil or blunt needle.

Tracing wheels are serrated wheels used with dressmaker's carbon. You lay your design over the fabric, with the carbon between the two, and run the tracing wheel over the lines. The serrations pierce the paper and leave a dotted line.

Traditional embroidery transfers are printed in reverse and then ironed onto your work, but they leave a dark line that will not wash out, so the stitching must be thick enough to cover the lines. Transfer pencils for drawing your own transfers of this kind are also available. Some commercially produced quilting transfers use a similar technique, but with silver lines, which show less but may still be visible after stitching.

PAPER
Use cartridge (sketching) paper, shelf paper, or artist's detail paper for planning designs, where several sheets can be taped together for working out very large patterns.

Graph paper is recommended for planning scaled patchwork designs and borders and for shaping templates. Isometric graph paper is helpful for constructing certain patchwork templates such as hexagons and equilateral triangles.

You will need tracing paper or tissue paper for transferring designs. Dressmaker's carbon paper is also used for transferring designs to fabric and gives a fairly long-lasting mark. It is available in several colors, including red, yellow, blue, black, and white. Choose the color nearest to your background fabric or thread, and also white (or other light colors), to show up on dark fabrics.

Notepaper is the ideal weight for backing papers used with hand-sewn cotton or silk patchwork. Thicker fabrics, however, may need slightly heavier papers. The paper should be sufficiently firm in order for its edges to be felt through the folds of the fabric.

CARDBOARD, ABRASIVE PAPER, AND ACETATE
Templates for all three techniques of quilting, patchwork, and appliqué can be made from these materials to suit your own designs. Thin ticket card (thin cardboard) is generally recommended for templates used in quilting and patchwork projects of average sizes. Abrasive paper (a fine sandpaper, for example) is especially good for gripping the fabric, but with repeated use, it has the disadvantage of wearing out at the edges. Both cardboard and abrasive paper templates can be strengthened with tape, and duplicates can always be made. For very large projects, where the

templates have to withstand repeated use, it is a good idea to use a more durable material such as acetate. This is available from art supply stores and can quite easily be cut to shape with scissors or a craft knife and ruler.

TEMPLATES

Quilting stencils are used in a similar way to templates for transferring designs to fabric. Although it is not difficult to make your own stencils from parchment, there are several traditional and modern designs available at craft suppliers. Templates for hand-sewn patchwork, such as shells, hexagons, and diamonds, can also be bought from craft stores in a range of sizes. They are made from thin metal or plastic and are produced either as two solid shapes, one ¼ in. larger than the other all around, or as a window template where the outer edge is ¼ in. from the inner edge. In each case, the larger shape is used to cut out the fabric and the smaller shape, or the inner edge, is used for cutting the backing papers. This gives a ¼ in. seam allowance all around the fabric patch. These templates can also be used for marking quilting designs.

Left: Paints and other design equipment can be very useful when designing your own quilt.

General Sewing Equipment

A good selection of pins is needed, including fine lace pins for delicate fabrics, dressmaker's stainless pins for general use, and glass-headed pins for pinning together several thicknesses. Being longer than average, the glass-headed pins are much easier on the fingers for pushing through bulky layers of fabric. You will also need a measuring tape and a dressmaker's tracing wheel for transferring designs, using the carbon paper method. Many craftworkers who do not use a thimble for ordinary hand-sewing will find that one, if not two, are essential for quilting. A second thimble is often used on the first finger of the hand under the frame to guide the needle back through the fabric. A 1 in. wide cotton tape is needed for stretching the layers of fabric into a quilting frame.

NEEDLES

Ordinary sharps and crewels are useful for most types of quilting, but some quilters prefer short "between" needles, which are more maneuverable. Straw and milliner's needles are extralong and so they are better for basting than for actual quilting.

Blunt-ended needles, such as tapestry needles, can be used for marking fabric (they make a faint indentation in the weave), and large-eyed needles and bodkins are very useful for threading the cords in corded quilting.

PINS

Ordinary glass-headed pins are fine for most jobs. However, you may want to buy some silk pins, which are extrafine, if you are working on silk, since they don't leave any marks on the fabric. T-pins are useful when you are machine-stitching.

FRAMES

Quilting frames are available in two broad types: round and rectangular.

Round frames are like large embroidery hoops and can be handheld or mounted on stands. They are used for stretching and stitching small projects or for quilting larger areas one bit at a time.

Rectangular frames are used for stretching larger quilts and can be flat or rolling: On flat frames, medium-size projects can be stretched flat; on rolling frames, the quilt is attached at both sides, then the area not being worked on is rolled onto the support at one side.

CUTTING EQUIPMENT

You will need a selection of scissors of different sizes: small, very sharp embroidery scissors with fine points for corded and trapunto quilting; ordinary small scissors for snipping threads; large scissors for cutting out fabric; and general-purpose scissors for cutting paper, templates, etc. You may also find that pinking shears are useful for finishing some areas.

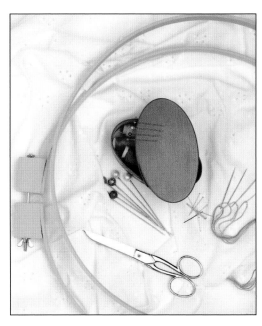

Above: Obtain a good selection of general-purpose sewing equipment and you'll have most of the items needed for quilting. You'll need needles of different sizes for quilting, embroidering, and finishing projects, and sharp scissors for cutting accurately. A quilting hoop is also useful to have.

USING A ROTARY CUTTER

The circular blade is very sharp, so always be sure to put the guard on when it is not in use. To prepare the fabric, fold and stack four to six layers together with raw edges even and the straight grain aligned. Steam press. Place them on the cutting board and first straighten one edge of the fabric by holding the ruler down firmly near the edge of the stack and running the cutter along the ruler's edge. Hold the blade toward the ruler and cut away from you. Now line up this straight edge with one of the grid lines on either side of the board or ruler and cut the required widths and lengths. Remember when cutting to include seam allowances of ¼ in. on each side of the patches or stripes; thus, for a finished square of 4 in., cut 4½ in. squares.

Before starting on a project with the rotary cutter, practice with scrap fabric to learn the technique. Keep the blade pressing against the ruler (it has a tendency to veer outward and away at first) and go slowly. Hold the ruler firmly. For certain projects the rotary cutter can more than halve the time spent preparing fabrics, so it is worth the small amount of practice required to learn the technique.

SEWING MACHINES

A sewing machine is an excellent labor-saving piece of equipment useful for quick quilting, piecing patchwork blocks, and stitching on appliqué patches, as well as

Below: Using a rotary cutter

for stitching very long seams needed for making up items and many finishing processes.

For best results, choose a machine that will give a good, straight stitch, and, if possible, with reverse stitch for starting and finishing and a zigzag stitch for applying fabric patches and quick seaming.

IRONS

An iron is an essential piece of equipment and a sound investment for any quilt-maker. A thermostatically controlled steam iron generally gives best results and is especially good for

pressing seams really flat. It is quite important to have your iron and board close to your sewing area so that you can get used to the professional technique of pressing seams as you sew.

TAPE MEASURE
An essential item in any workbox, most now have both imperial and metric measurements.

UNPICKER
This is more efficient than scissors for undoing small stitches.

WAX
This will prevent knotting and strengthen the thread when hand-stitching.

THREADS

Threads for Hand-Quilting
If you are quilting by hand, you can buy especially strong cotton-covered polyester quilting thread in a wide variety of colors. Heavy-duty mercerized cotton is also useful.

Ordinary sewing threads, silks, embroidery threads, and metallic threads can be used for small amounts of quilting or in short lengths; they tend to wear through and break more easily than quilting thread.

Threads for Machine-Sewing
Ordinary sewing threads are fine for straight quilting by machine, but if you want to use one of the thicker embroidery threads, make sure that your machine is suitable and your needle is big enough.

Special machine embroidery threads are ideal for satin stitch or close zigzag appliqué work, and many of the metallic threads on the market can be used in machines, too, as long as you use a suitably sized needle. An alternative is to use the thick thread in the bobbin and quilt with the right side underneath.

Transparent threads are available in two shades: a totally clear version for pale fabrics and a smoke-colored version for dark fabrics. These can be useful when you want the texture of quilting but don't want the stitches themselves to stand out.

Materials

The materials you can use for quilting are many and varied – in fact, you can quilt practically any material in one way or another! However, there are some fabrics, threads, and battings that are particularly useful, especially if you are a beginner, and using suitable materials for a given project will allow you to make the most of your quilting skills.

If you are new to quilting, begin your work with some of the standard materials, but don't be afraid to experiment; there is no limit to the beautiful and interesting effects that you can achieve by combining different quilting methods with the wide variety of fabrics and threads.

GENERAL-PURPOSE QUILTING FABRICS

The most popular fabrics for most types of quilting are fairly firm, closely woven ones that show quilted textures well without losing their own shape. Cottons are probably the most popular fabrics – choose close-textured fabrics such as dress cottons, poplins, and polished cottons. Polyester-cotton blends can be useful, but they look and behave a bit differently from pure cotton fabrics, so try not to mix the two types of fabric in the same project

unless you want to exploit their differences.

Silk is wonderful for quilting, but can be a bit slippery, so baste it firmly in place. Slubbed, habutai, dress-weight, and crepe de Chine silks are good choices. Linen, upholstery-weight cotton, and closely woven wools are good if you want a thicker fabric for quilting.

Satins, synthetic fabrics, metallic fabrics, and materials such as suede and fine leather can all be used in different ways. If you are making a project that will be washed, make sure that you choose washable materials throughout, since some fabrics shrink when washed the first time. It's a good precaution to wash them before you cut or stitch them to prevent any possible problems later.

For backing projects, either use the same fabric as you use for the top or choose a less-expensive version of a similar fabric, and remember to use firm fabrics to back trapunto quilting.

WADDING (BATTING)

The choice of a quilt filler (the warm interlining between top and backing) can be confusing because there are different types. How you plan to finish the quilt and the purpose for which it is made will affect this choice.

The most economical filler is the polyester wadding (batting), which is available in a variety of weights. For quilting by hand or machine, the 2 oz. weight is the most practical. Thin enough to stitch through easily while providing a warm, light interlining for the quilt, it is washable and will not shrink or disintegrate when used, even in small quilts. The heavier weights (3–6 oz.) are suitable for tied quilts and will give a puffy, scrunchy appearance to comforters. Another advantage to polyester wadding is that it is available in large pieces, big enough for king- and queen-size quilts, so there is no need to join pieces for these larger quilts. For smaller projects, wadding is also available in rolls of different widths. One disadvantage to polyester is that it will blunt scissor blades and machine needles quickly, but this is far outweighed by the advantages.

Needle-punched polyester wadding is more compact and solid, having been subjected to a flattening process under hundreds of needles, which reduces the thickness while maintaining the weight. Using this type of wadding creates a flatter effect, which is suitable for wall-hung quilts.

A cotton filler is the traditional material for quilts—originally teased and carded flat by the quilt-maker, it is now available preflattened and will give a flatter and more "antique" look to your quilt, but it is more difficult to work with. It comes off the roll folded with a papery outer skin and has to be opened out carefully to expose the loose fibers. As cotton will not hang together like polyester, it must be closely quilted to keep it in position. The manufacturers recommend that the quilts with cotton fillers be dry-cleaned; they cannot be preshrunk, as the filler would disintegrate.

Cotton Classic has overcome many of the disadvantages of pure cotton while retaining the quality of pure cotton wadding. It is 80 percent cotton and 20 percent polyester and has bonded surfaces, making it easier to handle. It can also be preshrunk: Put the wadding into a cotton

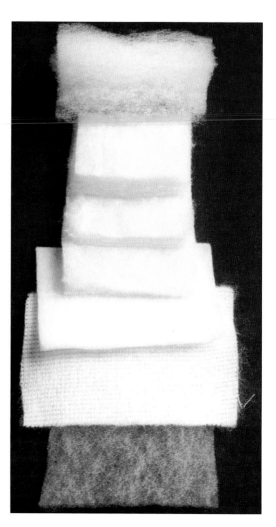

Above: A selection of different quilt fillers. From top to bottom: different weights of polyester wadding are available—this is the 4 oz. weight (1); silk in different weights (2, 3, and 4); Cotton Classic (5), a low-loft wadding; domette (6), a woven interlining suitable for wall hangings; needle-punch (7), a flatter polyester wadding.

bag (e.g., a pillow case), immerse in hot water, and then give it a brief spin in the washing machine. Now remove the wadding from the bag, shake it out gently, and hang it in a warm place to dry out. Some people like the slightly "antique" look that occurs when the finished item is washed and the wadding shrinks slightly, puckering the surface fabric.

Pure silk wadding is now available by the roll, and quilted with silk thread to give your quilt a luxury feel. However, it is expensive and is probably best reserved for small projects and garments.

Terylene, or cotton domette (sold as warm curtain lining), is a good filler for wall hangings and door curtains. It helps produce a flat surface and has a good weight.

Below: Braids, ribbons, and eyelet laces can provide the perfect finishing touches to your quilt. Sequins, buttons, beads, bows, and ribbon roses look very pretty when they're used for tied quilts, and cords of different thicknesses provide the texture in corded quilts.

Quilting Techniques

The guiding principles for quilt-making were that the quilt should provide warmth and protect the body and that old fabrics could be used again. These underlying guidelines have not changed, but the uses to which quilts are put — garments, bedding, and covers — have varied according to the needs and, later, the fashions of the times. The definition of quilting has, however, remained unchanged for thousands of years: It is the placing of a padding between two layers of material that are then held together with stitches.

The skill of the quilter was revealed not only in the stitching but also in the designing of the motifs and borders (especially the corners) to be quilted. Some women were so good at the designing that they were paid to design a pattern for others to use. The most popular designs were twists, chains, and feathers, which were used both as central motifs and for corners and borders.

Regional designs in Britain were made by fishermen's wives, who favored border patterns that looked like waves and a central motif of a horn of plenty or another symbol of safety from the sea. Later, quilting patterns were executed in wide horizontal stripes, not with a central motif with fillings and borders.

As quilting involves decoratively stitching together two or three layers of fabric using one or any number of techniques, examples of these are shown on the following pages.

Stitches

Although there are many stitches that can be used for quilting, including most outline stitches, many techniques use the same few basic ones. Hand-quilting stitches are used most often to produce a texture in the padded layers, rather than as a decorative feature in themselves. These days, of course, it is possible to work many quilting techniques by machine as well as by hand. Don't think of machine-quilting as a poor relation of hand-quilting – it has its own strengths, and versatile modern machines can produce unique effects that are impossible to imitate by hand.

HAND-QUILTING STITCHES

RUNNING STITCH
This is the most basic of all stitches and is the traditional stitch used when doing traditional quilting by hand. It can be used for many other techniques, such as contour quilting and random quilting. The needle is pushed in and out of the fabric using small, even stitches.

BACKSTITCH
Backstitch is excellent for producing the strong lines of stitching necessary for corded quilting and other techniques such as shadow quilting and trapunto, where an unbroken stitching line is needed. The needle is put into the fabric at the tip of the preceding stitch and emerges the same distance again along the stitching line.

CHAIN STITCH
Chain stitch can be used to provide a thicker, more decorative line than backstitch. The needle is brought to the front of the fabric, then reinserted at the same place, emerging further along the stitching line so that it catches a loop of thread to make one link in the chain.

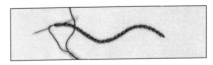

The three stitches you'll find most useful for quilting by hand are the running stitch (top left), backstitch (bottom left), and chain stitch (above).

OTHER USEFUL HAND-STITCHES

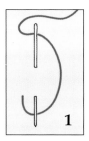
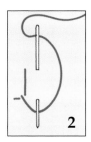

BLANKET STITCH

1 Bring the needle out just below the patch edge. Insert it through the material and bring out directly below, with thread under needle.

2 Repeat around the patch. Where possible, make sure that a single stitch goes into an angled corner and that the stitches are adjusted evenly around the outer corners.

3 To ensure continuity around the edge, finish the stitching by taking the needle through to the back at the bottom of the stitch.

FLY STITCH

1 Bring the needle out to the left, and holding the thread downward, insert the needle to the right. Make a diagonal stitch to the center and pull through.

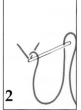
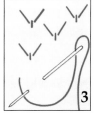

2 Hold the V-shaped loop down with a short, straight stitch and repeat as needed.

3 Work the stitches either close together around the edges of a patch or outside an embroidered line to soften the effect.

COUCHING

1 Bring out the thread to be couched on the right side, directly over the material edge you want to conceal.

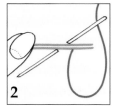
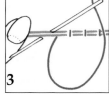

2,3 Hold thread down toward the left and bring out the couching thread below. Make a short, upright stitch into the material and bring out below the threads. Continue to make evenly spaced stitches.

QUILTING

1 Use a fairly short thread, about 20 in. Wax the thread and knot the end to prevent twisting. Bring the needle out and pull the knot through the backing, leaving it caught under wadding.

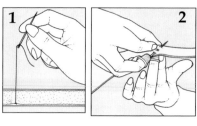

2 With a thimble on the second finger of the sewing hand, make several stitches. Keep the thumb pressed down on the fabric, just ahead of the needle, while the other hand below feels the needle and guides it back through.

MACHINE-QUILTING STITCHES

Machine-quilting is fast and direct and appeals to many contemporary quilters mainly because they can express their ideas quickly — and perhaps more spontaneously. Machine-quilting, however, produces a harder line and lacks the beautiful softness of hand-quilting.

Pin and tack the layers together as for hand-quilting and stitch the design, working outward from the middle. Use a medium-length stitch and loosen the tension if the wadding is very thick. You may also need a larger needle.

It may require several attempts and specific practice in order to stitch a line perfectly straight or to follow flowing curves and make neat circles. Use both hands to feed the fabric under the needle and do not stitch faster than you can comfortably control the fabric.

Finish the quilting and neaten the threads by first pulling them through to the back of the work. Thread them into a needle through the wadding, bring it out a short distance away, and cut close to the surface.

A quilting bar can be fitted to the sewing machine and provides an excellent guide for stitching parallel lines. After marking and stitching the first line, adjust the bar so that it rests on the previously stitched line.

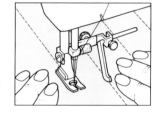

Using the quilting bar, complete the first line and repeat as needed. Stitch very long lines in alternate directions to avoid puckering underneath.

Above: Here are some examples showing both hand- (left) and machine-quilting (right) .

STRAIGHT STITCH

Straight stitch is ordinary machine stitching. It is used when you want a thin line of stitching that doesn't show too much, as in basic quilting or trapunto, and is also useful for quilting patchwork shapes.

SATIN STITCH

If you don't have a satin stitch option on your machine, set it to the closest possible zigzag stitch, which will have a similar effect. Use satin stitch for attaching the edges of appliqué shapes and for quilting thick, colored bars.

ZIGZAG

Zigzag is useful for making unusual quilting lines and also for quilting appliqué shapes that have been attached with transfer fusing web so that they don't fray.

Finishing Techniques

When quilting is complete, the edges must be neatened either by turning the raw edges of the quilt top and tacking them to the inside and then stitching together or putting a binding around the quilt to enclose the wadding and raw edges. The techniques shown here are some of the most popular finishing methods. Choose the one that you think will work best for each item that you quilt, and decide whether to use a matching, harmonizing, or contrasting color.

STRAIGHT BINDING WITH STRIPS

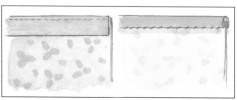

For invisible stitching, lay the strips of binding fabric on the quilt front, right sides together, and stitch by hand or machine along the seam line. Fold the binding over the quilt edge, turn under the seam allowance on the raw edge of the binding fabric, and slip stitch it neatly and invisibly to the backing fabric.

For one-seam straight binding, fold under both of the raw edges of the binding fabric and then fold the binding in half lengthwise. Slip the folded binding over the raw edges of the quilt and baste near the folded edges so that both the front and back edges are caught down, then stitch along this line by machine.

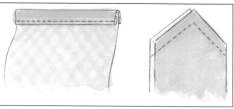

For mitered corners on both sides, cut and stitch the binding strips in the shape shown before applying to the quilt.

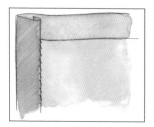

STRAIGHT BINDING WITH BACKING

When binding with backing fabric, make sure that your backing fabric is bigger than your top fabric. Press under the raw edge, then fold the fabric over the front of the quilt and stitch down by hand or machine.

For mitered corners on the front, trim the backing fabric across the corner as shown, then turn over and slip stitch the diagonal edges together before sewing the rest of the binding in place.

BIAS BINDING

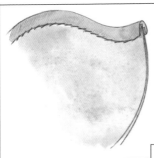

Purchased or handmade bias binding can be attached by hand or by machine in the same way as straight binding (see opposite page and above), but has the advantage that it can be curved around corners, so it is useful for binding curves and irregular shapes.

To make your own bias binding, mark diagonal strips at regular intervals across a large rectangle of fabric as shown, then join the straight sides, aligning the raw edge with the first pencil line in from the end at each end. Starting at one end, cut along the line and you'll create one long bias strip, which saves you from having to join individual strips all the time.

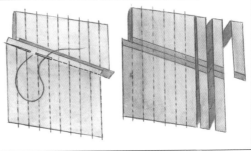

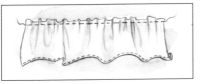

RUFFLES

For a single ruffle, turn a narrow double hem under along a gathered strip of fabric and sew it in place by hand, by machine straight stitch, or by machine blind hemming. Insert using either the second or third method shown in the lace and ribbon section on the next page.

For a folded ruffle, fold a wider strip of fabric in half lengthwise and gather it along the aligned raw edges, then use either the second or third method given in the lace and ribbon section below.

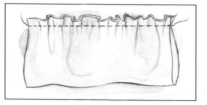

For a double ruffle, make two fabric ruffles of different widths or make one of fabric and

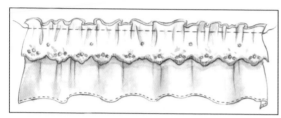

one of lace, eyelet lace, or ribbon, gather them together, and insert using either the second or third method given in the lace, eyelet lace, and ribbon section below.

LACE, EYELET LACE, AND RIBBON

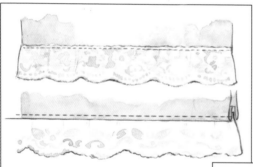

If the edge is neatly bound, you can simply attach it to the front of your hemmed quilt with slip stitch or machine stitching.

If you want to hide raw edges or gathers or prefer to finish your quilt edges at the same time, press under the raw

edges of the quilt and backing, baste the edging in between, and then stitch just inside the edge by hand or machine.

For invisible insertion, stitch the edging to the front of the quilt first, aligning the edge of the edging with the edge of the quilt so that the decorative edge is toward the center. Then turn the raw edge under to the back, press, and slip stitch the backing fabric to the underside of the edging.

CORDING

If you want to cord the edge of your quilt, cut a strip of bias binding the same measurement as the circumference. (If you are cording a straight edge, the fabric doesn't need to be on the bias.) Fold it over filler cord

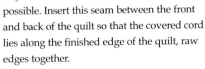

and stitch the two layers of the fabric together by hand or machine, as close to the cord as

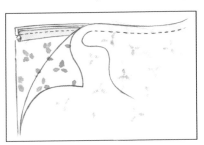

possible. Insert this seam between the front and back of the quilt so that the covered cord lies along the finished edge of the quilt, raw edges together.

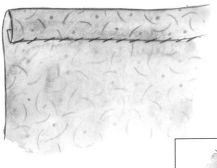

PLAIN HEMS

For a turned hem, press under a double hem to the wrong side along the raw edges and stitch it in place on the wrong side using slip stitches, hand-hemming stitches, or machine stitches.

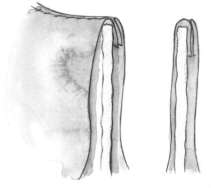

For hems on bulkier items, when you don't want to use a double hem on the raw edges, turn the edges of the front and the backing in toward the batting, folding one of the edges over the batting so that it is concealed. Stitch the two layers together by machine, or slip stitch or oversew the folds together.

Traditional Quilting

In its most familiar form, quilting consists of three layers of fabric: a top fabric, a backing fabric, and a layer of soft padding sandwiched between them. The three layers are held together with lines of stitching worked as a decorative pattern. Many of these patterns originated in the British Isles and were brought to North America by colonists. These traditional designs include flower shapes, other natural forms such as feathers and leaves, and geometric and interweaving border and filling patterns. American quilters have often incorporated such motifs in patchwork, using them to embellish the solid areas within a quilt. The stitching is usually worked in thread matching the fabric so that the stitches themselves are inconspicuous and the design is created by contrasting textures – although modern quilters are experimenting with variations on this tradition.

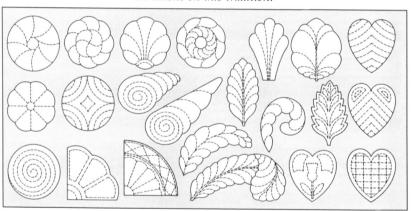

Above are examples of some of the traditional motifs of circles, flowers, leaves, fans, and hearts, used singularly or repeated to make composite shapes for central designs or corner motifs. Below are a selection of traditional borders often used as a continuous

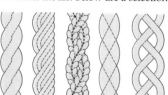  band around a design or combined with corner motifs.

Try adapting the true lover's knot design to a square quilt; enlarge the central medallion, then make a border of feather designs radiating from the corners. Fill in the background with diamond filling texture.

You can put texture behind the rosette design, too; in this example, small rosettes taken from the center of the main medallion have been placed in each corner of a square quilt, and the diamonds stitched in between. The edge is finished with a ruffle.

You can use the central medallion to decorate a circular pillow, finishing off the edge either with cording or with a gathered ruffle in the same fabric.

By working a design in blocks, you can construct a quilt of any size. Here the rosette medallion has been worked on six blocks. The entwined border has been used all around the edges of the quilt, changing the direction of the twists in the center of each side.

Although the traditional quilting method is a very old one, it is still a favorite with contemporary quilters. The examples shown here — both old and new — demonstrate its versatility.

Here, quilting has been combined with appliqué. The appliqué tulips are arranged on the background in a diamond pattern that is echoed by the quilted lines. Each corner also contains a quilted shape.

This beautiful modern quilt is stitched in white-on-white silk and makes use of an unusual arched pattern to link the leaf designs in the border.

This quilt shows a typical Amish design and color scheme, enhanced by careful hand-quilting in orange and purple thread.

The quilted item above is a nineteenth-century Persian bath mat. The quilting is worked in backstitch through cotton batting and the motifs and central medallion are embroidered in various colored silks.

The swallow jacket shown here looks as though it was stitched by an expert; in fact, it was the designer's first attempt at quilting. The big swallow shape was enlarged freehand from a picture, while the smaller ones were traced. The leaves for the borders were copied from the designer's tea set.

Contour Quilting

Contour quilting is the simplest possible type of quilting — you don't even need to transfer a design onto your fabric, because you just stitch along the lines of a printed fabric. When you're selecting a fabric for contour quilting, choose one that has obvious bold shapes that you can quilt around: stripes, plaids, and bold, splashy patterns look very effective. Some quilting shops sell fabric panels specially printed with patterns that can be quilted and then made into pillows, crib quilts, or even garments, and these make very good starter pieces if you are new to quilting. Contour quilting can be done by machine or by hand. If you are quilting by machine, use an ordinary straight stitch; if you are stitching by hand, use running stitch or backstitch.

This pretty crib quilt uses a preprinted fabric panel. These are available in various nursery designs. Alternatively, you could use an allover print, provided that the main motifs are of a good size. The same print on a related solid color could be used for curtains and pillows. Pregathered eyelet lace has been used to finish the edge of the quilt.

This very simple method of quilting can also be used for bigger projects: Choose printed sheeting in a pattern that matches your bedroom curtains or carpet to make a quilt for your own room; use a length of children's print to make a unique throw cover to brighten up a child's room; buy some square printed panels and quilt them in the same way to make pillow covers.

The main lines of the design can be quilted along by machine or hand and the basting threads removed.

The raw edges of the front panel and the backing fabric are pressed inward and the eyelet lace stitched in between them. The basting threads are then removed.

The beautiful printed fabrics available today can be used to produce very dramatic effects with contour quilting, but you don't have to limit yourself to using prints. Several of the examples here use designs that have been painted onto the fabric, then quilted.

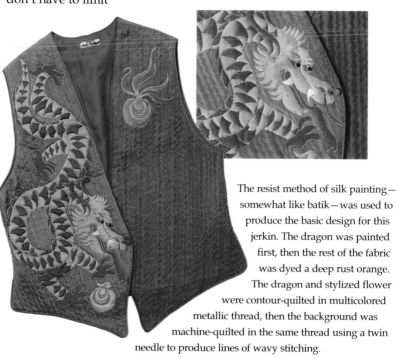

The resist method of silk painting—somewhat like batik—was used to produce the basic design for this jerkin. The dragon was painted first, then the rest of the fabric was dyed a deep rust orange. The dragon and stylized flower were contour-quilted in multicolored metallic thread, then the background was machine-quilted in the same thread using a twin needle to produce lines of wavy stitching.

The bow (right) was worked as a trial piece for decorating a crib quilt. The design was stenciled onto the background with fabric paint, then contour-quilted by hand over batting.

Printed fabric panels come in all shapes and sizes. This Christmas wreath was stitched from a preprinted panel over thick batting, then quilted by machine along the straight line of the design.

The irregular border was bound with red bias binding.

The delicate tones and shapes of the printed fabric on this pillow have been enhanced with contour-quilting by hand, producing a soft and gentle effect.

If you find patchwork a little daunting, cheat by using a preprinted panel. On this pillow panel the lines of the stars and squares were contour-quilted by machine before the pillow cover was assembled.

Shadow Quilting

Shadow quilting – like most other types of quilting – uses three layers of material, but this technique doesn't use batting. Instead, the patterns are produced by stitching pieces of contrasting fabric between two other fabric layers, the top layer being sheer or translucent so that muted versions of the colors beneath show through. The shapes of the pattern are emphasized by the lines of stitching around the inserted pieces of fabric, and if the fabric pieces are quite thick – felt, for example – the stitching produces an interesting texture, too. If you use sheer fabrics for the top and bottom layers, you can produce beautiful translucent curtains that will show off your designs as the light shines through.

Virtually any sheer fabric can be used for shadow quilting; although white is traditional, pastels and medium shades can produce unusual effects as they alter the colors of the materials underneath them. The examples on these pages demonstrate many different approaches to the basic shadow quilting technique.

A stencil effect has been used for this fruit bowl. The shapes for the bowl and the different fruits were cut from colored fabrics and fused to the background with transfer fusing web. The top was then covered in muslin to soften the colors, and each shape was stitched around in sewing thread in a matching shade. The irregular edge was bound with fine white bias binding.

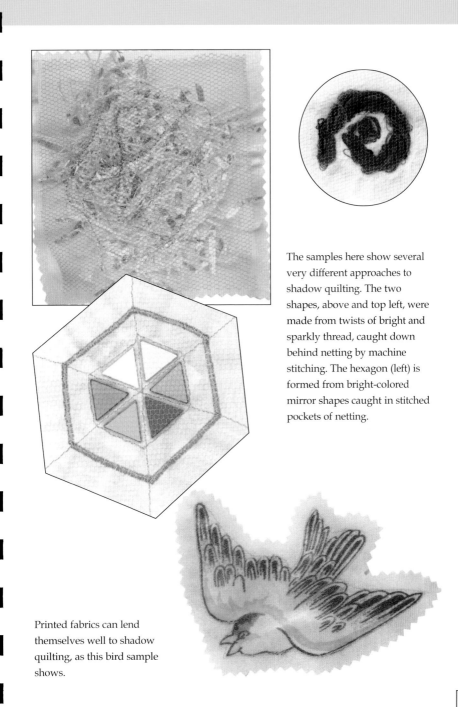

The samples here show several very different approaches to shadow quilting. The two shapes, above and top left, were made from twists of bright and sparkly thread, caught down behind netting by machine stitching. The hexagon (left) is formed from bright-colored mirror shapes caught in stitched pockets of netting.

Printed fabrics can lend themselves well to shadow quilting, as this bird sample shows.

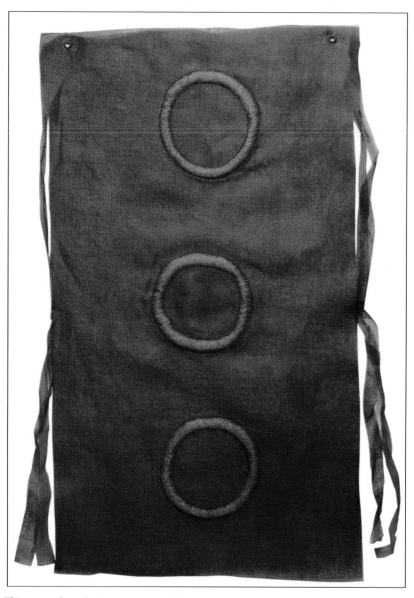

This unusual textile piece uses rings of rice captured in pockets of shaded muslin to produce a beaded effect; the designer was interested in using natural materials and experimented with lentils and other legumes, as well as rice.

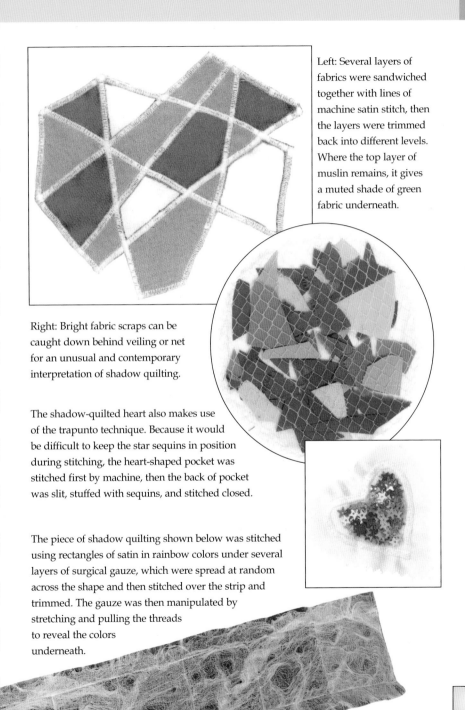

Left: Several layers of fabrics were sandwiched together with lines of machine satin stitch, then the layers were trimmed back into different levels. Where the top layer of muslin remains, it gives a muted shade of green fabric underneath.

Right: Bright fabric scraps can be caught down behind veiling or net for an unusual and contemporary interpretation of shadow quilting.

The shadow-quilted heart also makes use of the trapunto technique. Because it would be difficult to keep the star sequins in position during stitching, the heart-shaped pocket was stitched first by machine, then the back of pocket was slit, stuffed with sequins, and stitched closed.

The piece of shadow quilting shown below was stitched using rectangles of satin in rainbow colors under several layers of surgical gauze, which were spread at random across the shape and then stitched over the strip and trimmed. The gauze was then manipulated by stretching and pulling the threads to reveal the colors underneath.

Random Quilting

As its name suggests, random quilting doesn't follow a set pattern — you simply quilt in random shapes going across the item that you are working on. Random quilting is thus very easy to do and can be worked by hand or machine, yet it can result in some very sophisticated effects.

The technique can be used on all kinds of different fabrics and on different scales — from very small items to very large. You can work the stitches in the same color as the background fabric — so that the texture becomes the main feature — or you can use a contrasting or glittery thread so that the lines of stitching become decorative features in their own right.

Random quilting gains its effect from smoothly flowing lines; the exact arrangement they are in doesn't matter too much — what's important is that the lines be consistent in style. You can even do random quilting with angled lines, but again you need an overall consistency in the lines you use within one project.

Experiment with a number of alternative patterns (see examples below and on opposite page); they can be used for numerous projects, from belts and bags to whole quilts.

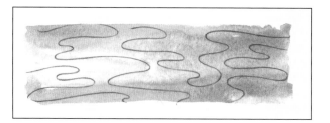

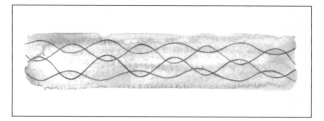

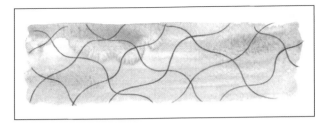

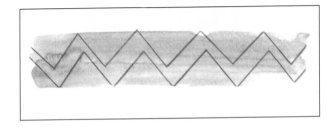

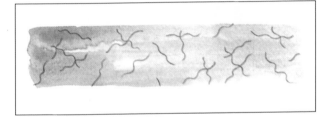

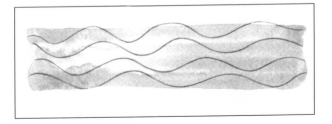

Random quilting is ideal for experimentation because the pattern created is entirely up to you. The pieces on the following two pages show the work of several quilters using random quilting in a variety of ways.

The jerkin above has been stitched so that it is reversible; all the seams are hidden and the random quilting lines look equally neat on both sides of the garment. Using this technique, you get two jerkins for the same amount of time and effort as it takes to produce one.

The so-called vermicelli, or meander, pattern involves quilting an item by stitching very wiggly lines in random patterns all over it. For the best effect, none of the lines should cross. This bag has been quilted with vermicelli stitch; the areas left plain form a secondary flower pattern.

The fabric used for this sumptuous evening jacket is gold-brown silk douppioni, quilted over batting. The jacket is covered with an asymmetric design of flowering leaves thrown into relief by the vermicelli quilting around them. The edges of the leaves have also been stitched with a very fine line of metallic thread.

This palm leaf panel (right) combines the stained glass appliqué technique with random machine-quilting. The green fabrics were basted into position on a padded background, then the leaf fronds were stitched in different directions before the lines of bias binding were added.

These quilted makeup bags were stitched as experiments in random quilting. The shapes were padded with thin batting, then quilted with random lines of chain stitch in rainbow colors. On the larger bag, random lines of white running stitch were added across the rest of the bag.

Tied Quilting

This technique gets its name from the old method of quilting by tying together several layers of fabric (you can still see a similar technique used on old mattresses). Originally the threads were tied so that little thread showed – the purpose was practical rather than decorative – but quilters soon began to see the decorative possibilities of the technique and incorporated buttons, little circles of leather or fabric, beads, or more ornate knots into the designs. Items of furniture such as tufted sofas use the same principle. Tied quilting is one of the most versatile of the modern quilting methods; several variations and possibilities can be seen on the following pages.

This kind of tied quilting is ideal for both small and large quilts. Instead of finishing the edge with pregathered lace, you could use eyelet lace or attach a single or double ruffle made of the background fabric (see pages 31 and 32).

You could also use bows to tie-quilt a suitable purchased quilt made with printed fabric, or try just quilting a full-size bedspread with bows in satin ribbon in the same color; this looks very pretty in white or cream, but can also look effective with dramatic colors such as midnight blue or dark crimson.

The following examples of quilts use the tied quilting technique.

Above, top: Apply the strips of lace diagonally and position the bows in a diagonal stripe in the opposite direction.

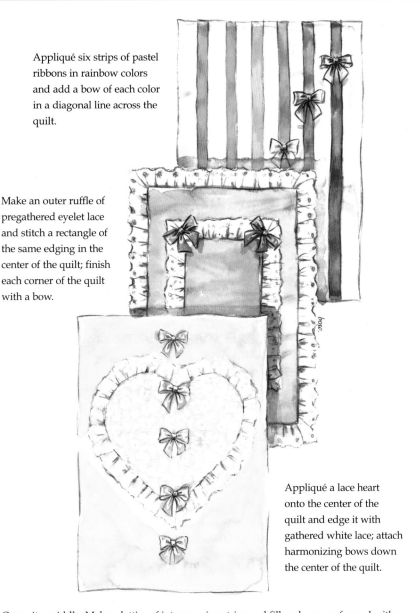

Appliqué six strips of pastel ribbons in rainbow colors and add a bow of each color in a diagonal line across the quilt.

Make an outer ruffle of pregathered eyelet lace and stitch a rectangle of the same edging in the center of the quilt; finish each corner of the quilt with a bow.

Appliqué a lace heart onto the center of the quilt and edge it with gathered white lace; attach harmonizing bows down the center of the quilt.

Opposite, middle: Make a lattice of interweaving strips and fill each square formed with a ribbon rosebud. Opposite, bottom: Appliqué strips of eyelet lace and thread them with colored ribbon; stitch matching bows onto the center of each strip.

Although tied quilting is one of the oldest quilting techniques, it can be adapted very easily to produce extremely modern-looking results, as you can see from the contemporary pieces shown on these pages.

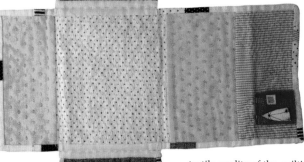

This textile piece was inspired by old domestic needle cases and uses household fabrics such as burlap and ticking, highlighted by everyday sewing items such as needles and scraps of embroidery. The stitching uses tied threads and beads as well as making use of conventional quilting. The designer intends for the piece to be handled so that the tactile quality of the quilting can be appreciated.

This shows the reverse side of the needle case and the tied quilting techniques used. The ties echo the ribbons used to tie up the needle case.

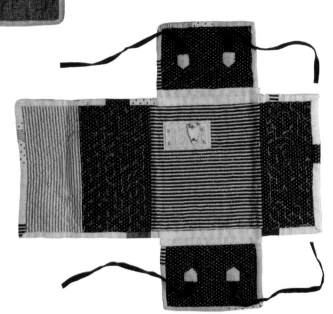

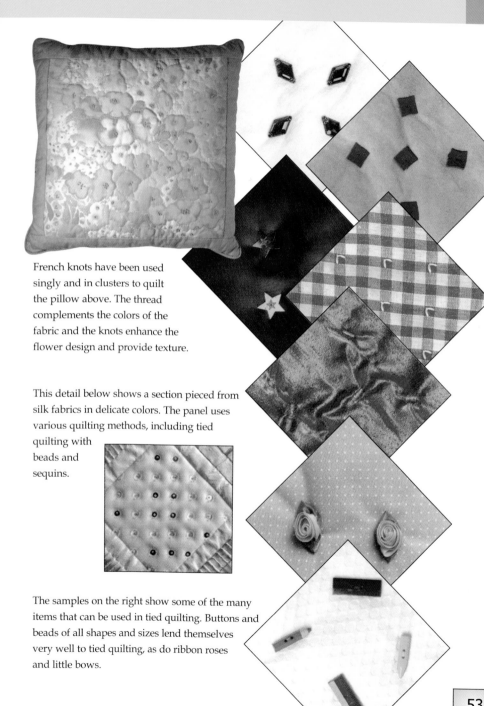

French knots have been used singly and in clusters to quilt the pillow above. The thread complements the colors of the fabric and the knots enhance the flower design and provide texture.

This detail below shows a section pieced from silk fabrics in delicate colors. The panel uses various quilting methods, including tied quilting with beads and sequins.

The samples on the right show some of the many items that can be used in tied quilting. Buttons and beads of all shapes and sizes lend themselves very well to tied quilting, as do ribbon roses and little bows.

Trapunto Quilting

Trapunto is also known as padded or stuffed quilting, which gives a good clue to the method used. Each area to be quilted or padded is first outlined with stitching, then the backing layer is slit to allow stuffing to be pushed into the space and the slit is then sewn up. Because of the slits made in the backing fabric, trapunto-quilted items should always be lined or used for projects in which the raw cut edges are safely concealed by an additional layer, such as a picture frame. Because you can vary the amount of stuffing used in each area, trapunto quilting can be used to produce some highly three-dimensional effects.

This technique gives one the opportunity to use more unusual fabrics, such as stretchy nylons and knits, velvets, velours, and taffetas, as well as the usual fabrics. For the backing, choose a soft, open-weave fabric such as muslin, scrim, or voile. When planning your design, each area to be padded must be completely enclosed to make a good shape.

This modern three-dimensional cushion takes padding a stage further. The knitted hand holding a tent-stitched miniature cushion conceals a greeting card pocket. Knitted stripes, felt leaves, and embroidered flowers decorate the surface.

TIPS
FOR PROFESSIONAL RESULTS WITH
TRAPUNTO QUILTING

• Cut out the main fabric and backing to the same size and transfer the design, in reverse, to the backing fabric using dressmaker's carbon paper.
• Place both fabrics wrong sides together, and working outward from the center, tack diagonally and vertically in both directions.
• Outline the design with small running stitches by hand or by machine, being careful to pick up both layers. Work from the center out.
• Remove the tacking threads and then, working from the wrong side, snip the backing in the middle of each area to be padded using small embroidery scissors.
• Using a round-ended bodkin or small crochet hook, stuff the shapes with teased-out wadding or scrim.
• Carefully mold each shape, periodically checking the effect on the right side. Finally, slip stitch the openings together and neaten the finished work with a lining.

The technique of trapunto quilting is used worldwide and is a good way of drawing attention to a central element in a design by making it three-dimensional on a two-dimensional background.

Here are some examples of trapunto in both traditional and contemporary designs.

These two examples come from the Far East and use the same trapunto technique. The central motifs— elephants—have been appliquéd onto the backgrounds in contrasting fabric, then stuffed to make them stand out from their surroundings.

This panel uses trapunto quilting to highlight the tulip petals and leaves. The three-dimensional white-on-white contrasts dramatically with the diagonal rainbow lines of embroidery and beadwork that are echoed in the surrounding edge.

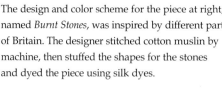

The design and color scheme for the piece at right, named *Burnt Stones*, was inspired by different parts of Britain. The designer stitched cotton muslin by machine, then stuffed the shapes for the stones and dyed the piece using silk dyes.

Corded Quilting

Also known as Italian quilting, corded quilting has actually been used in many European countries for several centuries. The name "corded" describes it exactly; the relief effect is created not by stitching layers of fabric together but by inserting cord or yarn in channels that have been stitched through two layers of fabric. The resulting raised lines cause the design to stand out against the flat background. Corded quilting is especially well suited to interwoven patterns, such as Celtic designs and knot motifs, in which the overlapping lines are enhanced by the cords threaded through them.

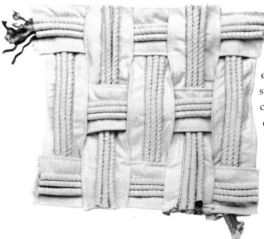

This is an example of experimental cording on narrow strips of calico. The strips are corded with hand-dyed piping cord before being woven and secured by hand, forming an unusual textured fabric.

Below: A border design of interlocking triangles that, when filled with cord, gives a pleasing contrast to the plain center.

Far right: An allover trellis pattern constructed with interwoven parallel lines.

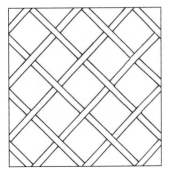

TIPS
FOR PROFESSIONAL RESULTS WITH
CORDED QUILTING

• Transfer your design to the backing fabric and pin the two layers together, right sides outward. From the center, tack diagonally and vertically in both directions, adding more lines of tacking on larger projects.

• Working on the wrong side, hand-sew around the design using small running stitches, being careful to stop and start new channels as suggested by the design. Simple designs can be machine-sewn.

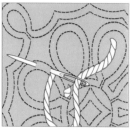

• With the wrong side facing, separate the backing threads or snip into the channel, and insert a bodkin threaded with quilting cord. It is best to have a short length of cord in the needle and not pull the cord too tightly. Pass through the channel a little at a time, bringing it out at angles and curves.

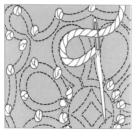

• Reinsert the needle into the same hole, leaving a small loop of cord on the surface—these will eventually become eased into the channels.

Corded quilting can be worked by hand or machine and is most suited to a closely woven top fabric and a loosely woven backing, as in padded quilting. Linen and linen scrim are the traditional fabrics used — these are hard-wearing and launder well — with a cotton cord or soft yarn for the quilting. Although piping cord now makes a good alternative, it gives a slightly harder effect. Incidentally, all cords should be washed first to prevent shrinkage later on.

Corded quilting is an ancient technique, but it has lost none of its appeal; today's quilters are still producing beautiful corded work and also experimenting with new effects.

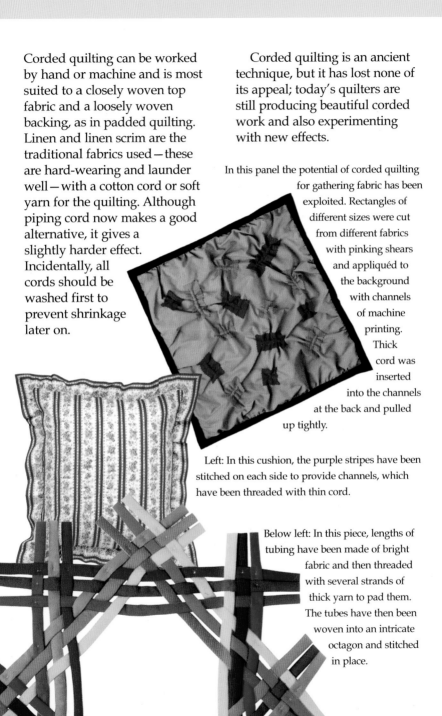

In this panel the potential of corded quilting for gathering fabric has been exploited. Rectangles of different sizes were cut from different fabrics with pinking shears and appliquéd to the background with channels of machine printing. Thick cord was inserted into the channels at the back and pulled up tightly.

Left: In this cushion, the purple stripes have been stitched on each side to provide channels, which have been threaded with thin cord.

Below left: In this piece, lengths of tubing have been made of bright fabric and then threaded with several strands of thick yarn to pad them. The tubes have then been woven into an intricate octagon and stitched in place.

Sashiko Quilting

Sashiko (pronounced "sash-ko") quilting is an ancient Japanese technique. Several thin layers of fabric are stitched together with running stitches in geometric patterns. Sometimes many different stitch patterns are used in one item, sometimes just one; but the stitching is worked out so that the threads themselves form the main pattern — they are not there just to provide texture. So, whereas in basic quilting the running stitches are often worked out as unobtrusively as possible, in Sashiko quilting they are larger and often worked in contrasting thread, each stitch twice as long on the front of the fabric as it is on the back. Sashiko quilting is sometimes padded with a thin layer of batting, but it can be worked with flat fabrics, too.

TIPS

• If you want to reduce bulk around the hem, turn it under just once and stitch it down with medium-length zigzag machine stitching or, if your sewing machine has the option, hemming stitch.

• Use a large, sharp needle for working the quilting, as you will need to make quite a large hole in the closely woven fabric in order to pull the cotton through.

Sashiko quilting is very good for garments, as you do not need bulky batting, so liven up a plain jacket or coat by quilting sections with geometric designs.

You can put lots of variety and texture into the stitching by using two different threads in the needle at once — for example, two colors of stranded floss or a pale matte cotton with a strand of darker silk, or a matte thread together with a strand of metallic thread.

Although Sashiko is a simple technique, the results it produces can be spectacular, as you can see from the number of contemporary Sashiko works on the next two pages. Intense color schemes seem to suit the opulence of the Japanese designs, with blue being an obvious favorite.

The pair of cuffs shown above have been stitched on gold silk using the wineglass pattern of overlapping circles; the cuffs are lightly padded for extra texture.

The wineglass pattern has also been used on this pillow cover. The circles have been carefully drawn onto the background fabric so that an even border of solid fabric is left around them at the edges of the cushion, then the lines have been stitched in white Sashiko quilting.

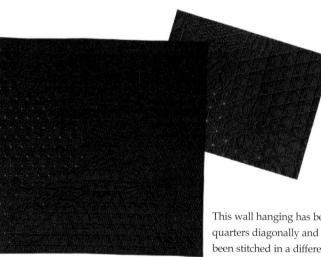

This wall hanging has been divided into quarters diagonally and each quarter has been stitched in a different geometric pattern. The strong diagonals are broken up by different Oriental motifs, each one basically circular, stitched in the same color scheme of white on blue.

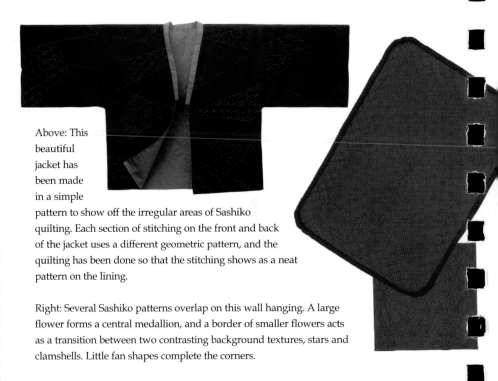

Above: This beautiful jacket has been made in a simple pattern to show off the irregular areas of Sashiko quilting. Each section of stitching on the front and back of the jacket uses a different geometric pattern, and the quilting has been done so that the stitching shows as a neat pattern on the lining.

Right: Several Sashiko patterns overlap on this wall hanging. A large flower forms a central medallion, and a border of smaller flowers acts as a transition between two contrasting background textures, stars and clamshells. Little fan shapes complete the corners.

Below: Sashiko quilting has been used to produce stitched detail on these two bags. The bag on the left has made good use of one self-contained motif, the fan, and the other uses a section of geometric design. At the edges each design has been stitched around with a double row of quilting for extra emphasis.

Quilting & Appliqué

Appliqué means "applied." In appliqué one fabric is stitched on top of another to produce a decorative effect. There are several ways of combining appliqué with quilting. Some methods involve stitching the appliqué fabric to a background first and then quilting around or near it, while with other methods it's possible to use the same stitching to secure the appliqué fabric and quilt the item at the same time. Appliqué opens up infinite possibilities for varying the texture, color, and finish of your quilted items. With so many different fabrics available today — from the sheerest voiles to thick upholstery fabrics — it's a fascinating way to explore the creative possibilities of quilting.

Essentially, appliqué is a two-dimensional technique that may be strictly functional, such as a knee patch on a pair of jeans, or purely decorative, such as a satin motif on a negligee. However, in picture making and more experimental work, it can be a vital art form in which personal statements are expressed. The play of light on surfaces, stitching, and subtle modeling of fabric may all be exploited to create work with immensely tactile qualities.

FABRICS

Almost any material can be used in appliqué, and like patchwork, a varied selection is often a stimulating source of design inspiration. Your ultimate choice should be governed by what you plan to make, bearing cleaning requirements in mind. For practical items, the fabric needs to be easy to handle and either washable or suitable for dry cleaning. While felt and lace scraps, for example, are excellent for picture making, they would not wear well on children's jeans that have to be regularly laundered.

With delicate fabrics and those that fray easily, such as some silks and satins, a lightweight iron-on interfacing is recommended for extra support. Designs are transferred (in reverse) to the interfacing, either before or after ironing it to the wrong side of the fabric. The applied fabrics should not be heavier in weight than the ground fabric, although a second (finer) supportive layer can be added to the background if needed.

One of the main features of appliqué is making fabric "work" not just in color and shape but in pattern and texture. Patterned fabric, for example, can be used to suggest all kinds of images and textures, such as stripes for plowed fields, flower sprigs for gardens, pile surfaces for animal fur, and checks for bricks.

TIPS
FOR PREPARING TO
APPLIQUÉ

• Draw around the template on the wrong side of the fabric.

• Cut out, allowing a ¼ in. seam turning; clip inward curves.

• Turn the raw edges in and tack down the turning.

• Pin and tack, then stitch down.

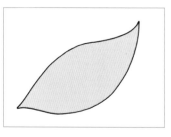

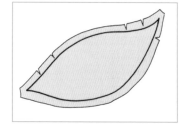

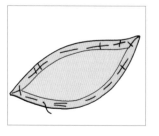

When you have chosen your project and have started laying the pieces of material to be appliquéd onto your background fabric in a pleasing arrangement, it is a good idea to secure them with a single stitch while you are working on other areas. Also, quilting small, shaped areas can be tricky, so turn your machine speed to slow and manipulate the fabric carefully so that you stitch smoothly around the edges.

Appliqué is a very versatile craft, and as the examples show on the next few pages, it can be used to stunning effect when teamed up with quilting. If your finished item needs to be hard-wearing, the raw edges of the fabric must be firmly stitched, but if your creation is purely decorative, anything goes!

Appliqué perse was used for this jacket; scraps of printed fabric were cut to shape and then appliquéd onto a black background, padded, and quilted with metallic thread. Bugle beads and tiny insect beads add the final touches.

Left: *Garden Wreath,* a nineteenth-century quilt. The quilt is divided into a number of blocks and shows appliquéd spray and block wreath patterns combined with patchwork maple leaves. (*The American Museum in Britain*)

The modern musical *The Lord of the Dance* was the inspiration for this panel, made in five sections. The quilter dyed some of the fabrics herself to achieve specific effects, then quilted the pieces by hand and machine.

The design of this dramatic quilt is based on a rose window in Chartres Cathedral. The stained glass effect is captured by the luminous printed fabrics, the black background fabric, and appliquéd black bias strips.

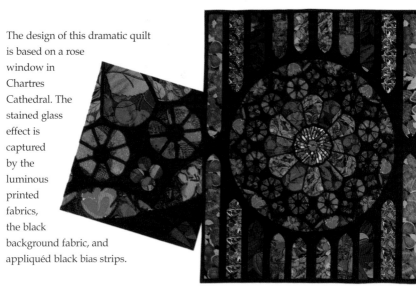

Quilting & Patchwork

We're all familiar with the term "patchwork quilt." This form of bedcover has, for centuries, been the most popular way of combining the skills of quilting and patchwork. There are, however, many other ways of putting the two skills together. Generally, the fabric pieces for the patchwork are joined, or "pieced," before being quilted, but some techniques allow you to do the two jobs together. You can quilt either in or alongside the seams in the patchwork, or you can stitch an independent quilting pattern around or across the patchwork, perhaps reflecting or repeating one of the shapes of the pieced fabrics.

AMERICAN BLOCK PATCHWORK

American block patchwork uses repeated shapes that, when put together, form the basis of a quilt design. The blocks can be purely patchwork, appliqué, quilting, or a combination. It is said that this method of making a quilt evolved when American quilt-makers had little space in which to work and each block was made individually on the lap and stacked away until enough were completed to be stitched together. This avoided the inconvenience of having an ever-growing sheet of patchwork in the limited space available. When blocks are placed edge to edge, interesting secondary designs appear, often merging the separate blocks into a complex overall design.

PATCHWORK BLOCKS

There are many patchwork, or "pieced," blocks, often with individual names such as Bear's Paw or Sherman's March. Each block requires one or more templates—the master pattern pieces from which the fabric patches are cut. Patches are placed with right sides of the fabric together and sewn with a small running stitch by hand or machine.

MAKING TEMPLATES

Rather than tracing templates from books and magazines, it is far more versatile and just as easy to make your own. This will give you freedom to adapt traditional block designs and enable you to change the size of a block, add a border where appropriate, and combine features from more than one design.

TIPS
FOR PREPARING
AMERICAN BLOCK PATCHWORK

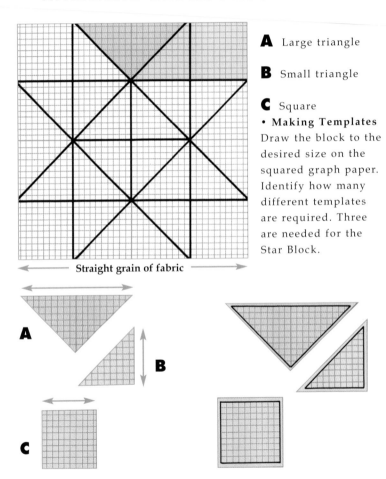

A Large triangle

B Small triangle

C Square

• **Making Templates**
Draw the block to the desired size on the squared graph paper. Identify how many different templates are required. Three are needed for the Star Block.

Straight grain of fabric

• From the full-size drawing, cut out each different shape that makes up the design and stick them onto stiff cardboard.
• For machine-stitched American Patchwork, add a ¼ in. seam allowance to the templates.

The square is one of the most basic and simple patchwork shapes. But there are many other shapes used, such as rectangles, that are not often used for allover patterns, with the exception of one called Hit and Miss, which can also be made using squares. Log Cabin, Pineapple, and Courthouse Steps are considered allover patterns, even though they are made up of squares in the same way as crazy patchwork. The reason for this is that the patterns do not stand up by themselves, but depend on the way that individual pieces are placed next to the other pieces to create the allover patterns that give rise to their names.

Above: This 1992 quilt was inspired by Amish bar quilts. The strip patchwork has a center square and random pieced borders. The wool and corduroy fabrics give depth of color.

Other shapes for patchwork include triangles, diamonds, and hexagons — all simple geometric shapes.

Triangles in a Flying Geese pattern form a traditional design, with the large triangles in dark colors and the smaller ones in light colors. The triangles are sewn with dark wholecloth strips in between. This 1991 quilt is an effective example of a strip patchwork quilt.

Right: An eight-pointed star made from diamonds.

Below: A sample of hexagons in a wave pattern.

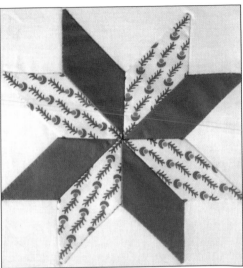

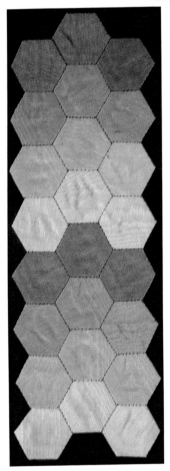

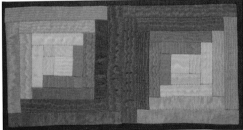

Above: An example of the Log Cabin pattern.

Right: Printed blue and plain white fabric was used in this curved design with an allover effect of mosaic tiles.

For this quilt, called *Myomi*, a commercial pattern was used for the blocks. The pattern was pieced by machine and then

quilted by hand, filling in the background of each block with a diamond design.

Right: This sawtooth design was produced by stitching strips of patchwork triangles between the alternate stripes of red and white. The quilt was made in the 1880s and is some kind of commemoration—the white stripes are covered with signatures.

Quilting Projects

Generally, the projects in this next chapter are arranged from the easiest technique to the more difficult, but each project has full instructions, so as soon as you've mastered the basic principles of quilting, you should be able to produce any of the items featured. In this section you'll also find inspirational items that will whet your appetite for taking each technique further in your own projects.

In this section there are twenty-two projects, each using one or a combination of the different techniques covered in the last chapter:

TRADITIONAL QUILTING
1. Nautilus Tea Cozy
2. Classic Pillow Covers

CONTOUR QUILTING
3. Place Mats

SHADOW QUILTING
4. Greeting Cards
5. Water Lily Curtain

RANDOM QUILTING
6. Mirror Frame
7. Clutch Purse

TIED QUILTING
8. Baby's Jacket
9. Baby's Coverlet

TRAPUNTO QUILTING
10. Rose Picture
11. Rainbow Cushion

CORDED QUILTING
12. Chinese Headboard

SASHIKO QUILTING
13. Spring Wall Hanging

QUILTING & APPLIQUÉ
14. Nightgown Case
15. Bright Rug
16. Quilted Play Mat
17. Stained Glass Quilt

QUILTING & PATCHWORK
18. Christmas Tree
19. Striped Jerkin
20. Pencil Case
21. Card Trick Shoulder Bag
22. Wave Pillow

Nautilus Tea Cozy

White-on-white is a very elegant color scheme, and it complements the clean lines of this nautilus shell design perfectly. With no extra patterns to distract attention from the shape, the beautiful curves of the shell flow into one another. You can either work the quilting on the front of the tea cozy and leave the back plain or reverse the image for the back so that the shell curves in the same direction on both sides.

PREPARATION

Enlarge the chart to the correct size using the grid method. This design gives a tea cozy 16 in. wide, but if you want a slightly bigger or smaller one, adjust your chart size and the amounts of fabric and batting accordingly.

Press the polished cotton pieces and muslin.

Pattern for the nautilus design

QUILTING

1 Mark the pattern on the right side of one of the white cotton fabric pieces with the water-soluble pen.

2 Place one of the pieces of muslin on a flat surface and cover it with one of the pieces of batting; place the marked fabric, right side up, on top of the batting. Baste the three layers together in a spiral of basting stitches from the center outward.

3 Beginning in the center of the design, quilt the shape along the marked lines.

If you are quilting by machine, use a very slow speed and short, straight stitches for the very center of the design, turning the fabric very carefully to follow the curves exactly. Increase to a medium-length straight stitch as you reach the second spiral of the design. Finish off each line of stitching neatly and securely at both ends.

If you are quilting by hand, quilt along the marked lines in small, even running stitches or backstitches.

1 in.

FINISHING

4 Remove the basting threads and lightly sponge away any pen marks with a clean, damp cloth.

5 If you are stitching a shell on the other side of the tea cozy, reverse the image and repeat steps 1–4 on the other piece of white cotton. If you want the back of the tea cozy to be plain, simply baste together the white cotton, batting, and muslin pieces.

6 Trim the front of the tea cozy so that you have an even curve around the top edge of the shell, 2 in. from the stitching line. Lay the front and back pieces together with right sides facing and trim the back to the same shape. Trim the remaining two pieces of white cotton fabric to the same shape.

7 With right sides together, pin, baste, and machine-stitch the front to the back along the curved edge, 1 in. in from the edge. Trim the seam and turn the tea cozy right side out.

8 Put the other pieces of white cotton together with right sides facing and stitch a 1 in. seam from the base to about 6 in. up each side of the curve.

9 Slip this lining over the tea cozy, right sides together. Pin, baste, and machine-stitch the straight seam along the base of the tea cozy, then turn it right side

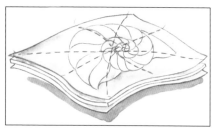

The design is traced onto one piece of the white cotton using a water-soluble pen. The batting is sandwiched between the white cotton and the muslin.

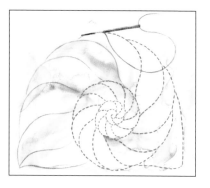

The main lines of the design are quilted by hand or machine; the pen lines will have already begun to fade, and any remaining marks are removed with a damp cloth.

out through the gap in the lining seam.

10 Neatly slip-stitch the gap in the lining seam closed, tucking the lining in to the inside of the tea cozy as you do so.

Classic Pillow Covers

These two pillow covers have been quilted in pretty pastels, using updated versions of traditional designs. The pink pillow design features a central rose motif surrounded by a wavy Celtic-inspired border that twists and untwists over itself. The green pillow design has a central Celtic knot and is surrounded by a border of feathers — very common quilting motifs. The background of the green pillow cover has been given an overall texture with a checkered pattern. Such filling patterns are often used in traditional quilting to enhance and provide a contrast to the larger, more intricate patterns of the main motif.

PREPARATION

Press the polished cotton and muslin squares.

Enlarge the patterns (see overleaf or pages 210–11) onto large sheets of paper.

Mark pattern A on the right side of the pink cotton square and pattern B on the right side of the green square.

QUILTING

1 Lay the squares of muslin side by side on a flat surface, cover with the squares of batting, and lay the marked squares right side up on top of the batting. Baste all three layers together in a crisscross pattern.

2 If you are quilting by machine, stitch along the lines of the designs with straight stitches, using matching thread. If you are quilting by hand, quilt along the lines of the designs with small, even running stitches.

3 Remove the basting threads.

FINISHING

4 Trim the edges of the squares evenly so each measures 18 in. square. Cut the corners of the pink pillow cover so that they are rounded.

Above: The marked fabric, batting, and muslin are sandwiched together and held in place with crisscross lines of basting. The lines of the design are then quilted using matching thread and either straight machine or small running stitches, then the basting threads are removed.

See patterns in larger detail on pages 210 and 211 in Patterns section.

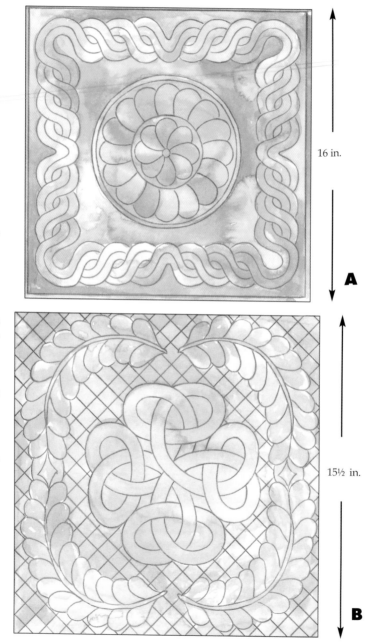

16 in.

A

15½ in.

B

5 If you are cording the edges, cut the bias strips from your matching fabrics, cover the filler cord, and stitch the cording in place around the edges of the quilted shapes.

6 Press under and stitch a narrow double hem along one of the long edges of each of the backing panels. Trim the corners of the opposite long edges on the pink panels so that they match the corners of the quilted front of the pink square.

7 Place the quilted squares right side up on a flat surface and lay the matching backing panels on top of them, right side down, aligning them with the edges of the squares with the hemmed edges overlapping. Pin and baste them into place along the seam lines.

8 Stitch twice around the raw edges of each square, taking a 1 in. seam allowance.

9 Trim the seams and the corners of the pillows, cutting them diagonally, then turn each cover right side out.

Above: The quilted fabric is trimmed to shape on the pink pillow front and the corners are rounded off. Then the backing panels are hemmed, each along one edge, then stitched to the pillow fronts, right sides together, hemmed edges overlapping.

Place Mats

*Use contour quilting to make a unique set of place mats for your dining room.
Choose a fabric that matches or complements your decor — perhaps the
same fabric as your draperies or upholstery — and cut out sections that
you can then quilt and bind. All the mats can be the same, or you
can quilt different sections of the pattern for each mat.*

MATERIALS

For each mat you will need:

1 piece of printed fabric, 14 x 20 in.; remember to allow extra if you want to use a particular part of the design

1 piece of solid-colored backing fabric, the same size as the printed fabric, in a harmonizing color

1 piece of thick polyester batting, the same size as the printed fabric

Matching sewing thread

PREPARATION

Wash and press the top and backing fabrics.

Enlarge the mat pattern onto stiff paper and cut it out to make a template.

QUILTING

1 Choose the shapes on the fabric design that you want to appear on the finished mat. Lay the fabric right side up on a flat surface and position the template on the fabric so that the shapes fall where required. Use a soft pencil to draw around the edge of the template.

2 Cut around the mat shape, ⅜ in. outside the pencil line. (The pencil line will act as your stitching guide for the seam line when it is time to attach the binding.)

3 Cut the backing fabric and the batting to the same shape as the patterned fabric.

4 Place the backing fabric right side down on a flat surface, position the batting on top, then lay the printed fabric, right side up, on top of the batting. Baste all three layers together with several lines of basting stitches in both directions.

The mat shape is marked on the fabric, allowing you to make sure that the chosen motifs are arranged as desired in the right positions.

5 If you are quilting by machine, stitch along the main lines of the design using a medium-length straight stitch. Begin with the shapes nearest the center of the mat and work outward. Finish off the ends of each thread neatly and securely. If you are quilting by hand, quilt along the main lines of the fabric design using short, even running stitches. Begin with the shapes nearest the center of the mat and work outward.

FINISHING

6 Remove the basting threads.

7 Finish the raw edges of the mat by stitching the bias binding over them, using the pencil line on the right side as a stitching guide. (See page 31 for methods of attaching bias binding.)

The fabric is cut ⅜ in. outside the marked line, leaving the pencil line as a stitching guide for the bias binding.

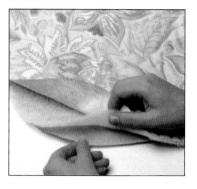

The mat shape is basted to the batting and backing fabric and the main lines of the design are stitched along by hand or by machine.

Left: A pattern for the place mat

TIPS
FOR ENLARGING DESIGNS

• Use the enlarging feature on a photocopier. If you do not have ready access to a photocopier, print shops offer this service for a reasonable charge.

• The traditional grid method is free but takes longer. Either draw a grid or use graph paper and trace the design. Then, on a larger piece of paper, draw a larger grid or use the larger squares on the graph paper and simply copy the lines in each original square in the equivalent square on the larger grid. If you start with ½ in. squares, 1 in. squares on the second sheet will double the measurements of the original; 2 in. squares will make them four times as big, and so on.

VARIATIONS

The opulence of a rich Oriental print is enhanced by the use of gold metallic thread used in running stitches along the main lines dividing different areas of the pattern. Because the print is asymmetrical, stitching these lines produces an attractive and informal quilted design.

On the rainbow mat, the main lines of the motifs are stitched by hand, using running stitches sewn in white thread. The mat is edged in bright blue bias binding—picking up the blue in the rainbows and clouds—stitched on by machine in blue straight stitches so that the stitching doesn't stand out.

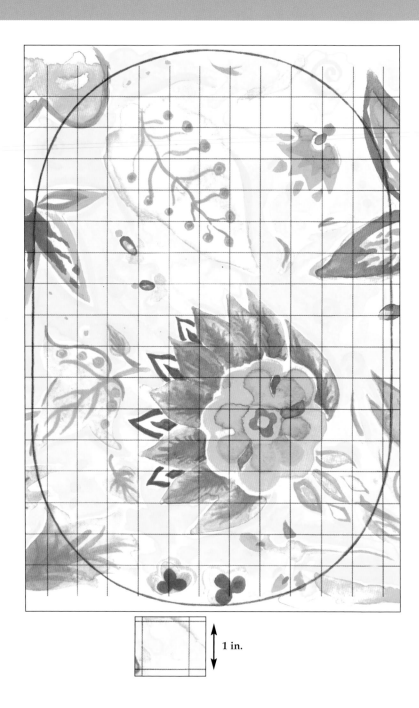

1 in.

Greeting Cards

Hand-stitched cards are perfect for special occasions such as birthdays, anniversaries, weddings, or the arrival of a new baby. The two designs here are versatile, and they can be produced using scraps of fabric from your sewing chest. Use a very sheer fabric for the top layer — such as a very fine organdy, organza, or firm chiffon — to allow the colors underneath to show through as much as possible. Blank greeting cards are available in many different sizes, colors, and shapes, so choose a card that goes with the fabric scraps you have, or buy a white card and paint it yourself.

MATERIALS

FOR THE GLITTER CARD

1 cream-marbled blank
greeting card
1 piece of gold glitter fabric, the
same size as the folded card
1 piece of sheer fabric, the same
size as the folded card
Scraps of metallic fabric in pink,
turquoise, and royal blue
Metallic threads to match
the fabrics
White all-purpose glue
Transfer fusing web or glue stick

FOR THE CANDLE CARD

1 blue blank greeting card
Scraps of felt in royal blue, pink,
yellow, orange, and red
Sewing threads in the
same colors
1 piece of white fabric, the same
size as the folded card
1 piece of sheer white fabric, the
same size as the folded card
White all-purpose glue
Transfer fusing web or glue stick

GLITTER CARD PREPARATION

Press all the pieces of fabric that you are going to use.

If you are going to use transfer fusing web, iron a small section 1 in. square onto the back of the pink, blue, and turquoise glitter fabrics. Cut small triangles out of each of these fabrics, two of each color (if using bonding web, cut the triangles where it has been attached).

If you are using fusing web, peel off the backing paper, position the triangles where you want them, and iron them to secure them to the gold background fabric. If you are not using fusing web, glue the triangles in place with the glue stick.

QUILTING

1 Place the sheer fabric over the gold background fabric and baste firmly in place so that it won't move during the stitching.

2 Stitch around the edges of the triangles with matching metallic thread, using backstitch and leaving a small margin between the edge of the triangle and the stitching line.

FINISHING

3 When you have completed the stitching, remove the basting threads and press the design on the back, making sure the iron is not too hot.

4 Spread a little glue over the inside of the fold-down flap on the card and a little bit around the inside of the window section (don't use too much glue on the window frame or the card may buckle).

5 Position the quilted fabric carefully face down on the glued window section so that the design shows through the window. Spread the fabric as flat as possible.

6 Fold the glued flap over the back of the design and weigh the card with a heavy book until it is dry.

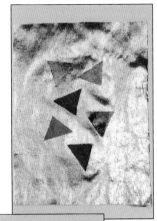

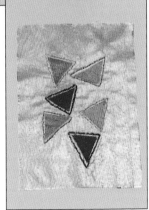

Top right: The triangles are cut from the glitter fabric and glued in place on the gold background fabric with transfer fusing web or glue stick.

Middle: The sheer fabric is laid over the top of the triangles and the layers are basted together to prevent them from slipping.

Bottom right: The triangles are stitched down with glitter thread and the basting threads are removed.

CANDLE CARD PREPARATION

Press the fabrics you plan to use.

Trace all the shapes shown in the pattern (shown on opposite page) onto thin paper and cut them out for use as templates. Choose a different number instead of "1" if appropriate.

If you are using fusing web, use the paper templates as guides for cutting out pieces. Iron these onto the felt scraps of the appropriate colors and cut out the shapes. If you are not using fusing web, use the paper templates as guides for cutting out the felt shapes.

If you are using fusing web, peel off the backing papers, position the felt shapes on the white background fabric, and iron them on to secure them in position. If you are not using the fusing web, glue the felt pieces in place with dabs of glue stick.

QUILTING

1 Baste firmly around the edges of the fabrics so that the felt shapes will not move; where there is more than one layer, work a line of basting stitches across the design as well.

2 Using matching threads, hand-stitch around the edge of each felt shape, starting with the number and the center of the flame and working out. Use backstitch to produce a solid-colored line.

3 When stitching is complete, remove the basting threads and press the design on the back.

FINISHING

Finish the card in the same way as the glitter card.

TIPS
FOR PROFESSIONAL RESULTS

• Where you have several layers of felt, stitching the central motif first (for example, the center of the flame) helps to prevent the sheer fabric from distorting.

• If you want to emphasize the colors of your shadow fabrics, stitch around the shapes in thread the same color as each shape, or darker. If you want a more subtle effect, stitch around all the shapes in white.

Use these patterns as a guide for any number on the candle card.

Water Lily Curtain

Brighten up a dull view with a translucent curtain worked in shadow quilting. The subtle colors of the water lilies are ideal for this delicate design. Choose lightweight fabrics for the colored shapes – light satins, cottons, and chiffons, for example – so that they don't distort the background fabric. For the curtain itself, choose a semisheer fabric such as muslin or a closely woven organdy.

MATERIALS

2 pieces of semisheer white fabric to fit your window (the fabric pieces need to be exactly the width you want the finished curtain — ideally with selvages at the sides — and 2 ft. longer, to allow extra for hems and a ruffle)

1 piece of pale cream fabric, about 12 x 16 in.

1 piece of pale pink fabric, about the same size as the cream fabric

1 piece of pale green fabric, about 12 x 18 in.

1 piece of green fabric, about the size of the pale green fabric

¾ in. wide ribbon in cream and pink, as long as the width of the semisheer white fabric

Sewing threads to match the cream, pink, and green fabrics

Sufficient transfer fusing web to cover the colored fabrics and the ribbons

Scraps of fabric in dark cream and pink

If you prefer, you can use printed fabric for making the water lily shapes, but not all prints are suitable. Choose a fairly small floral or repeat design so that its lines don't detract from the simple cut shapes, and choose one that's printed in fairly pale colors; otherwise you'll get strange-shaped silhouettes when the light shines through the curtain. Printed fabrics can add an extra touch of visual interest if you select them carefully.

PREPARATION

Wash and press all the fabrics.

Cut the white fabric pieces to the depth of your window and keep the remaining strips for the ruffle.

Trace the water lily pattern pieces onto thin paper and cut them out. Use these to cut four of each pattern piece out of the fusing web.

Iron the fusing web pieces onto the backs of the colored fabrics as appropriate and cut out around the shapes. Use the pale cream and pale pink fabrics for the main petals and the darker cream and pink for the top petals. Cut two large and two small leaves from each shade of green.

Lay one of the pieces of white fabric right side down on a flat surface. Peel away the backing paper from the fusing web and position the petal and leaf shapes in a pleasing arrangement. When you are happy with the design, iron firmly across the shapes to bond them to the background fabric.

Cut ¾ in. wide strips of fusing web, iron them to the back of the ribbons, and attach them to the lower edge of the white fabric in the same way.

QUILTING

1 Place the other piece of white fabric, right side up, on top of the bonded pieces. Baste the layers firmly together with lines of basting stitches across the width of the curtain.

2 If you are quilting by machine, use straight stitch and matching thread to stitch around the edges of each colored shape; tie the threads firmly on the wrong side of the curtain.

If you are quilting by hand, use backstitch and matching thread to sew around the edges of each colored shape; tie the threads firmly on the wrong side of the curtain.

3 When all the quilting is done, remove the basting threads.

FINISHING

4 If you have selvages at the edges of your curtain, baste the top and bottom layers together and stitch together by machine.

If you have raw edges, either bind them with straight strips of your white fabric or turn them under and machine-stitch a tiny seam.

5 Press ¾ in. to the wrong side along the top of the curtain, then press this under again to form a hem of about 2 in. Machine-stitch along the inner folded edge to make a casing

through which the curtain rod can be threaded.

6 Use some of the remaining white fabric to make a ruffle — single, double, or folded (see pages 31–32). Hold the curtain up to the window and measure it to see how deep the ruffle needs to be.

TIP
FOR A PROFESSIONAL RESULT

• If the fabric you have chosen for the curtain front and back loses its shape easily, as loosely woven muslin does, you can make it firmer by fusing the two layers together with ordinary fusing web across the whole area of the curtain before stitching, or you can spray the finished quilted curtain with firm starch.

Left: The pattern pieces backed by fusing web are positioned on the background fabric to form a pleasing design, then ironed to fuse them into position. The front piece of fabric is then placed over the fused design and basted in place.

Each colored section of the design is then stitched around by machine or hand using matching thread.

1 in.

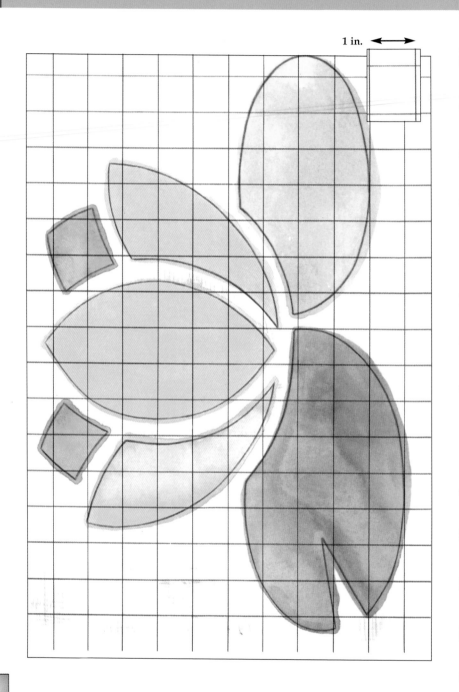

Mirror Frame

The use of couching (the technique of catching down a thick thread with a thinner one) allows you to use multicolored glitter yarn for this project. The colored lurex threads in the glitter yarn catch the light in a very attractive way. If you can't get a fine glitter yarn in the color you want, you can always use a thicker one – even very slubby ones will work well, since you don't have to stitch them through the fabric.

• 6. MIRROR FRAME •

MATERIALS

1 mirror tile or piece of mirrored glass

2 pieces of blue satin fabric, each 2 in. larger all around than the mirror

1 piece of muslin, the same size as the satin

1 piece of thick polyester batting, the same size as the satin

1 spool of blue glitter yarn

1 spool of Madeira gold machine thread or gold Gütermann sewing thread

Sewing thread to match the satin

1 piece of strong mounting board, the same size as the mirror

Clear tape

Strong craft glue

Craft knife

Water-soluble pen

Gold cord sufficient to finish the mirror (optional)

PREPARATION

Iron the blue satin and muslin.

Measure 3 in. in from each side of the piece of board and draw an inner rectangle. Cut it out using the craft knife, leaving a frame of board.

Lay the board frame on the right side of one of the pieces of satin, leaving the 2 in. margin all the way around. Draw around the edge of the frame—inside and outside—with a water-soluble pen, to create a frame shape/outline on the fabric.

Mark random wavy lines across the fabric with the water-soluble pen; these will be your stitching guides. Don't worry about spacing them evenly, as random quilting of this kind looks best when there is a good variation in the distances between lines.

QUILTING

1 Lay the piece of muslin on a flat surface, place the batting on top, then put the marked satin, right side up, on top of the batting. Baste all three layers together outside the marked lines (in case the basting leaves any marks on the satin).

2 If you are quilting by machine, thread the needle and bobbin with the Madeira gold thread and set the machine to a narrow zigzag stitch (about

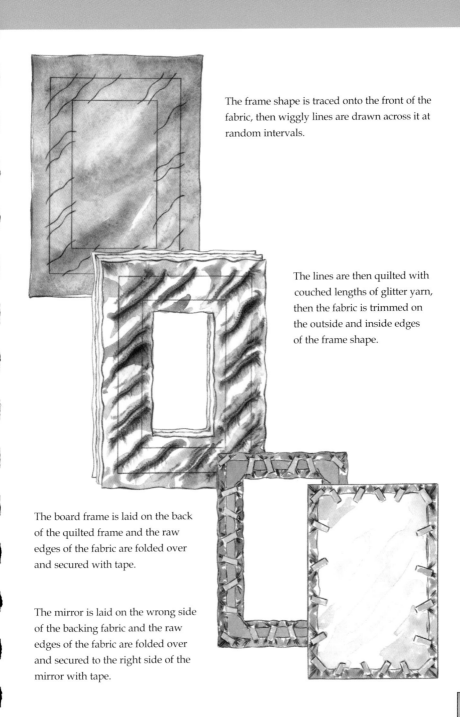

The frame shape is traced onto the front of the fabric, then wiggly lines are drawn across it at random intervals.

The lines are then quilted with couched lengths of glitter yarn, then the fabric is trimmed on the outside and inside edges of the frame shape.

The board frame is laid on the back of the quilted frame and the raw edges of the fabric are folded over and secured with tape.

The mirror is laid on the wrong side of the backing fabric and the raw edges of the fabric are folded over and secured to the right side of the mirror with tape.

¹⁄₁₆ in. wide and ¹⁄₁₆ in. long). Place a length of glitter yarn along each marked line and couch it down onto the satin with zigzag stitching, extending the stitching about ³⁄₈ in. over the edges of the marked borders.

If you are quilting by hand, use the Gütermann gold thread to couch the lengths of glitter yarn down onto the satin along the marked lines, using single stitches at short intervals. Extend the stitching about ³⁄₈ in. over the edges of the marked borders.

3 When the couching is complete, remove the basting threads and trim the fabric to within 1 in. all around the border, inside and outside. Using a damp cloth, gently wipe away any pen lines that are still visible.

FINISHING

4 Place the quilted border face down on a flat surface and position the board frame on top, leaving open margins of fabric all around it.

5 Fold the raw edges of the fabric over the frame and secure them with short pieces of tape, folding the corners around neatly.

6 Place the other piece of satin right side down on a flat surface and put the mirror on it, right side up, leaving an even margin all the way around.

7 Fold the raw edges of the fabric over the edges of the mirror and secure them neatly with short pieces of tape.

8 Spread a generous amount of glue on the back of the frame and place it on the mirror, making sure you match the edges of the two shapes. Leave it to dry thoroughly, weighting the frame slightly so that the surfaces are pressed together.

9 Use the matching blur thread to neatly slip-stitch the two layers of fabric together around the outsides of the frame.

10 If you wish, use craft glue to glue a border of gold cord around the inside and/or outside of the frame.

VARIATIONS

The same technique can be used for mirrors of all shapes and sizes, including oval and circular, and fancy shapes such as hearts. Make sure that you cut an even border shape on the mounting board by tracing around the mirror shape and measuring in evenly from all sides. Instead of blue satin, you can choose fabric—either solid or printed—that matches your room or upholstery. You can also work the frame in contour quilting instead of random quilting. Random quilting can be used in many patterns besides wavy

TIPS
FOR PROFESSIONAL RESULTS

• Don't be tempted to cut out the central panel of the satin before you have worked the quilting; keeping the center in helps keep the fabric from distorting during stitching.

• Working the couching a short way over the drawn borders helps ensure that the ends of the threads are safely hidden behind the frame when it is mounted, as they are then taken to the back of the board as you turn the fabric over and tape it down.

• If you prefer to stitch your mirror frame by hand, couch down the glitter yarn with a series of short stitches worked in plain gold thread. You can space them either evenly or at irregular intervals to emphasize the random nature of the design.

lines. Try working straight lines at random intervals or in different directions, for example, or stitch one long wavy line outward in a spiral pattern.

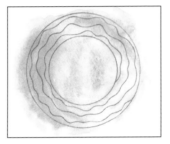

Above: One long wavy line is stitched in a random spiral around a circular frame—beginning in the center and working outward to the edge.

Below: A square mirror frame is stitched across at random intervals with straight lines of quilting worked at different angles. A pattern like this produces unusual effects where the lines cross.

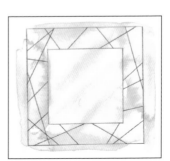

Clutch Purse

This sparkling evening bag makes use of the technique of reverse appliqué. Several layers of fabric are stitched together, then the layers are cut back to reveal different colors. The technique gives the layers a slightly three-dimensional effect, which is then enhanced with lines of random machine-quilting. This project is best stitched by machine, as the appliqué fabrics need to be securely fastened to the background to make sure that they will not fray. When assembled, the bag is finished with a handle made from tubing cut out of one of the appliquéd fabrics.

MATERIALS

1 piece of background fabric,
24 x 12 in.

2 pieces of similar fabric in
harmonizing colors, each 16 x 12 in.

1 piece of lining fabric, the same size
as the background fabric

1 piece of extrafirm iron-on stiffener,
the same size as the background fabric

1 piece of Stitch-N-Tear®, the same
size as the harmonizing fabrics

1 piece of thick polyester batting, the
same size as the background fabric

Sewing thread in harmonizing colors:
1 spool of decorative thread for the
appliqué, 1 spool of thread to match
the background fabric

Bias binding strips, 1 in. wide and a
total of 6 ft. long, made from the
surplus of one of the appliqué fabrics

Small button mold for covering

PREPARATION

Enlarge the pattern for the bag
and cut the shape for the back
and flap from all three fabrics, the
batting, the lining, the iron-on
stiffener, and the Stitch-N-Tear.

Cut the bag front from the
remaining background fabric, the
remaining lining, and the batting.
Mark the lines of the appliqué
pattern on the right side of the
background fabric flap,
preferably with a fading pen.

Lay the piece of Stitch-N-Tear
on a flat surface. Place the other
two layers of fabric, one on top
of the other, right sides up, and
position the background fabric
over the top. Baste all four layers
together.

Using straight stitching on
your machine, stitch around the
outlines of the appliqué pattern.

Carefully cut through one or
more layers of fabric close to
the machine-stitching to reveal
the different colors. Pull off the
Stitch-N-Tear.

QUILTING

1 Mark the fold line of the flap
on the iron-on stiffener and
work a line of machine straight
stitching along it (this will ensure
that the flap folds easily).

2 Place the stiffener on a flat
surface and cover it with the
matching piece of batting.

Position the appliquéd fabric, right side up, on top, and baste the layers together.

3 Set the sewing machine to satin stitch or a close zigzag, using the widest stitch setting, and thread it with the decorative thread. Stitch along the appliquéd outlines.

4 Baste together the front pieces of batting and background fabric.

5 Working straight machine-stitching in the harmonizing thread, quilt random lines across both pieces of the bag, working across the bag shape from side to side.

FINISHING

6 Baste the quilted shapes to the linings and trim any untidy edges.

7 Bind the straight top edge of the front section with some of the bias strip (see page 30).

8 Position the bag front so that it matches up with the lower edges of the bag, lining sides together, and baste right at the edge of the bag shape. Machine-stitch the two pieces together.

9 Make a small length of bias tubing from the remaining bias binding for a loop fastening and a longer one for the handle.

10 Bind right around the bag, inserting the handle ends at the edges where the flap folds,

and the smaller loop at the center bottom of the flap.

11 Cover the button with one of the appliqué fabrics and sew it in place on the bag front.

TIPS
FOR MAKING AND USING TUBING

• Fold in the raw edges to the wrong side along each side of the bias strip and fold it in half so that the folded edges are aligned, then machine-stitch or hand-stitch close to the folded edges.

• To attach a button loop and bias binding together, lay the binding along the edge of the quilting, right sides together and raw edges aligned. Slip the measured loop between the quilting and binding, bending it to form a U shape. Align the raw edges of the tubing strip with the raw edges of the quilting. Baste and sew in place in the normal way to attach the binding, but sew back and forth over the button loop ends to make sure that they stay secure during use.

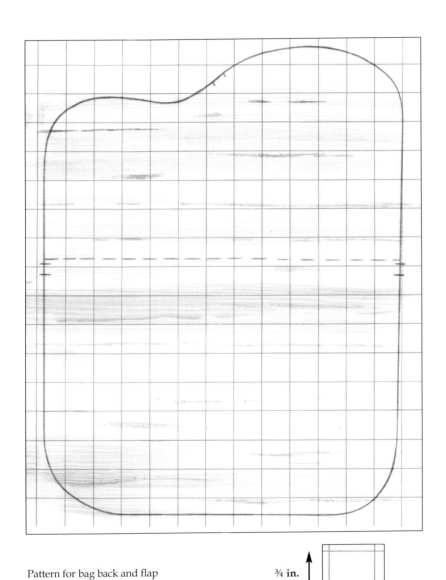

Pattern for bag back and flap

¾ in.

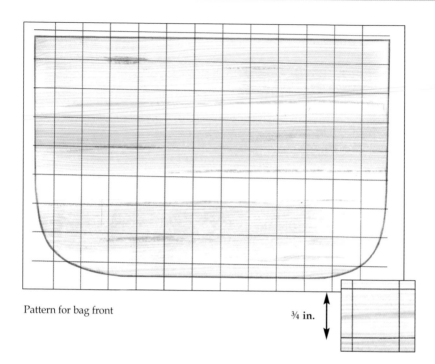

Pattern for bag front

¾ **in.**

The fabric layers for the bag and flap are stitched together around the outside, then lines of straight stitching are worked in random patterns across the flap.

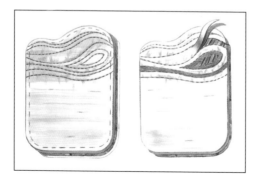

Fabric layers are cut back between the lines of stitching to reveal the different colored shapes underneath.

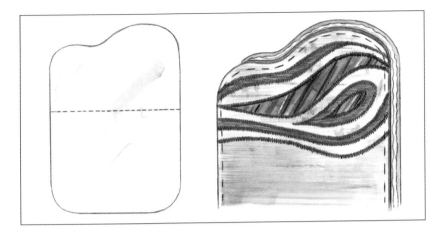

The extrafirm stiffener is stitched along the fold line to make it easier to fold the flap over when the bag is quilted.

When the appliquéd piece, batting, and backing fabric have been basted together, the edges of the cut layers are sewn together with bands of machine-stitching in decorative thread.

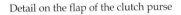

Detail on the flap of the clutch purse

Baby's Jacket

Quilted baby jackets are always fashionable and practical for chilly days. This roomy pattern will fit babies of about six to nine months. As the baby gets bigger you can roll down the sleeves. The pattern is simple, making it quick to assemble. Bias binding around the edges solves the problem of having to put seams into quilted pieces. The fabric chosen here has a little strawberry print, but many other prints or solids can be quilted in the same way. Choose a lining fabric that picks up one of the colors in the print.

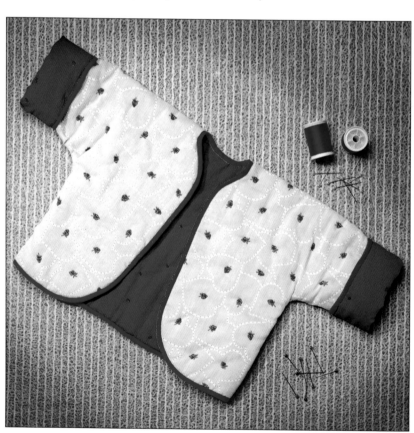

MATERIALS

1 piece of printed cotton fabric,
28 in. square

1 piece of thick polyester batting, the
same size as the printed cotton

1 piece of solid harmonizing cotton
fabric for the lining, the same
size as the printed cotton

Bright bias binding, ¾ in. wide
and 2 yd. long

1 skein of bright pearl cotton

Sewing thread for the seams and
attaching the bias binding

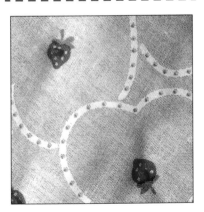

PREPARATION

Wash and press the outer and
lining fabrics.

Enlarge the jacket pattern to
the correct size onto plain paper
or dressmaker's grid paper, and
cut it out. Use the paper pattern
to cut out the printed cotton, the
solid cotton, and the batting. Cut
each fabric piece ¼ in. larger than
the paper pattern, as quilting the
pieces will reduce their overall
size a little. Cut the batting ¾ in.
smaller all around than the fabric
pieces.

With right sides together, pin,
baste, and machine-stitch the
underarm seams of the printed
fabric, taking a seam allowance
of ¾ in. Clip the seams and turn
the fabric right side out.

Stitch the underarm seams of
the lining fabric in the same way,
but don't turn the lining right
side out.

Butt the underarm edges of
the batting and baste them
together lightly with one or two
overcasting stitches, just to hold
the edges together.

QUILTING

1 Slip the batting inside the
printed jacket shape and the
lining inside the batting. The
seams of the outside and the
lining should now be hidden.
Baste all three layers together

firmly with lines of stitching at regular intervals.

2 Work French knots in the center of each strawberry or other motif by making a tiny backstitch in the lining behind the motif to secure the thread, passing the needle through to the front in the middle of the motif, but not bringing the needle all the way through. Then wind the thread around the needle several times, pull the needle through, holding the wound thread in place, and fasten the knot to the fabric by passing the needle back through to the lining side as near as possible to where the needle originally came up. Finish off the back of each knot neatly, since the stitches will show as a feature on the lining.

FINISHING

3 If necessary, trim the raw edges of the jacket shape so that they are even. Beginning at the center back of the jacket hem, attach one length of bias binding around the raw edges of the hem, fronts, and neckline.

4 Attach bias binding around the cuffs in the same way.

5 Remove the basting threads.

TIPS
FOR PROFESSIONAL RESULTS

• When you have slipped all three layers together, pin them together all over before you baste, just to make sure that the batting is evenly distributed without any lumps and bumps.

• If you want a substantial French knot, use about five winds of the thread around the needle; if you want a more low-key effect, use just three or four winds.

• If you don't want the quilting stitches to show on the jacket lining, make a lining in muslin first of all, and use that as the inside layer while you are working the quilting. Then just slip the cotton lining inside the jacket before you attach the bias binding.

With the right sides together, the sleeve seams of the printed fabric are stitched and clipped.

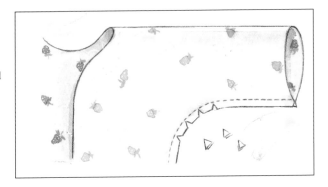

The underarm seams of the lining are sewn and clipped, the underarm edges of the batting are lightly held together with overcasting, the batting shape is slipped inside the printed fabric shape, and the lining fabric shape is slipped inside the batting shape.

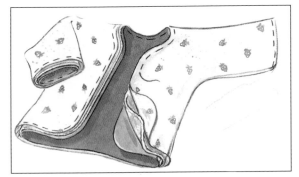

The center of each strawberry is quilted through all layers with a French knot in pearl cotton.

The raw edges are enclosed with contrast bias binding.

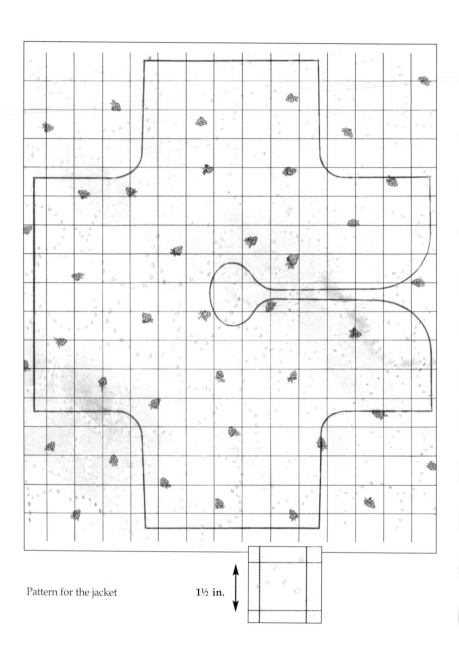

Pattern for the jacket   **1½ in.**

Baby's Coverlet

Rows of pretty cream lace on a cream background, highlighted with satin bows. This baby's quilt looks really special, but is very easy to make. The lace strips are appliquéd onto a plain background by machine, then the layers are quilted by sewing on bows. You can tie them yourself from satin ribbon, or save some time and buy them ready-made. For extra speed, buy pregathered lace for the edging ruffle.

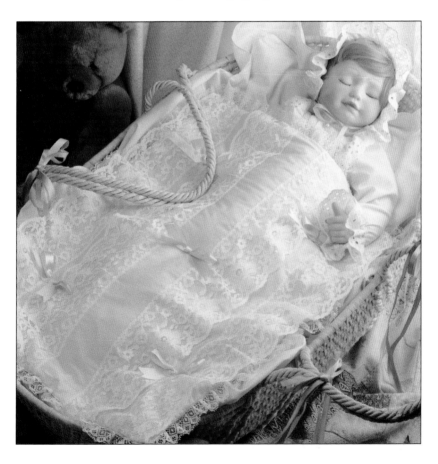

MATERIALS

2 pieces of cream cotton, polyester-cotton, satin, or silk fabric, 18 x 23½ in.

2 layers of thick or extrathick polyester batting, 16 x 22 in.

Cream lace, about 3 in. wide and 2¾ yd. long, preferably with one scalloped edge

Pregathered cream lace, about 1½ in. wide and 2½ yd. long

Cream satin ribbon, ¾ in. wide and 2 yd. long, or 5 cream satin bows. Bows and ribbon rosebuds come in many styles and colors; hunt around in fabric stores to see what is available

Matching sewing thread

PREPARATION

Wash and press the cream fabric.

On the right side of one of the pieces of cream fabric, measure 3¾ in. in from each long edge and mark the lines in fading or water-soluble pen. Measure another 3¾ in. in from each of the first lines and mark two more lines.

Cut four 24 in. lengths of the wide ungathered lace and pin the straight edges of the lengths along the marked lines on the fabric. Baste them in place, then stitch them by machine close to their edges. Remove the basting threads.

With the free edge of the lace lying toward the center of the rectangle, pin, baste, and machine-stitch the edge of the gathered lace ¾ in. in from the edges of the quilt top on the right side, pleating the lace at the corners so that it fits well.

Place the other piece of cream fabric on top of the quilt front, right sides together. Pin, baste, and machine-stitch a 1 in. seam around the edge, leaving a gap of about 6 in. along one of the short sides so that the quilt can be turned right side out.

Turn the quilt right side out and insert the two layers of batting, pushing them into the edges and corners of the quilt so that they lie flat. Turn the edges of the gap to the inside and slip-stitch them together neatly.

QUILTING

1 Pin the layers of the quilt together at regular intervals so that the batting doesn't slip.

2 If you are not using bows, cut the satin ribbon into five 14 in. lengths and tie a small bow in each.

3 Attach each bow to the quilt top with several strong stitches, making sure that each stitch goes through all the layers of fabric to produce the quilted effect.

FINISHING

4 Cut the free ends of the bows to the required length, cutting a V-shape out of them to prevent them from fraying.

TIPS
FOR PROFESSIONAL RESULTS

• If you find it tricky pleating the lace at the corners of the quilt, cut each corner of the fabric to a rounded shape; then you can simply stitch the lace around the curve. Remember to trim the batting to the same shape before you insert it.

• When you're making bows, it can be frustrating trying to get the satin side to show on each loop and free end. You can solve this problem by tying two loops together in an overhand knot to form a bow instead of making the bow in the conventional way.

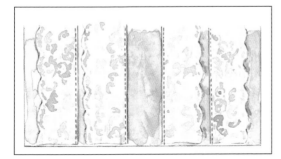

Four rows of wide lace are machine-stitched to the front fabric of the quilt at measured intervals.

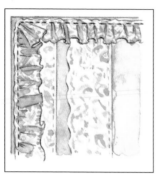

Left: The gathered lace is pinned, basted, and machine-stitched around the edges of the quilt front, with the free edges of the lace laid inside the edges of the fabric.

Right: With the right sides together, the quilt back is stitched to the quilt front around the edges, leaving a gap along one end so that the quilt can be turned right side out.

Left: The batting is slipped inside the quilt and the gap is slip-stitched together.

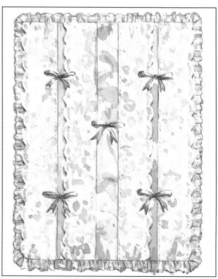

Right: If bows are not used, satin ribbon is cut into lengths and tied into bows. The bows are then sewn into place on the quilt front, stitching through all the layers. The ends of the bows are trimmed into V-shapes.

Rose Picture

The flowers and leaves in this picture are based on the stylized roses designed by Charles Rennie Mackintosh at the turn of the century. The flowing lines of art nouveau lend themselves well to embroidery. This project is a combination of trapunto and shadow quilting, for the top layer of fabric is sheer so that the colors of the stuffing show through. The marbled effect is achieved by stuffing the stitched areas with scrim, roughly cut pieces of thread in different colors and thicknesses.

10. ROSE PICTURE •

MATERIALS

1 picture frame, approximately
10 x 12 in.

1 piece of white mounting board, the
same size as the frame

1 piece of firm white organdy or
organza, 14 x 16 in.

1 piece of firm white cotton fabric, the
same size as the organdy or organza

Sewing thread in pink and green, or
if you are quilting by hand,
stranded floss or pearl cotton

Threads in different shades of pink
and green and different thicknesses,
for stuffing

Masking tape or clear tape

Soft pencil or water-soluble
or fading pen

Bodkin

Very sharp embroidery scissors

PREPARATION

Make two batches of scrim—one pink and one green—and mix each batch well to avoid large chunks of color, but keep one part of each batch of scrim very light in color.

Press the fabrics.

Enlarge the pattern to the correct size onto paper. Lay the organdy or organza over it and trace over the lines of the pattern using a soft pencil. (If you are quilting by hand, use a water-soluble or fading pen, as the drawn lines won't be so well covered by the stitching.)

QUILTING

1 Place the white cotton fabric right side up on a flat surface and lay the marked fabric on top of it, right side up. Baste the two layers together around the circle and around the flower and leaf shapes.

2 If you are quilting with a machine, thread your machine with pink thread and set it to close, narrow zigzag, or satin stitch, about ⅛ in., and stitch along each of the lines of the rose, finishing off each line carefully. Rethread the machine with green and stitch along the lines of the leaves, stems, and tendrils.

If you are quilting by hand, stitch along the lines of the rose in pink thread in close backstitch and finish off the ends of each line of stitching firmly. Do the same in green along the lines of the leaves, stems, and tendrils.

3 Press the embroidery flat.

4 Using the embroidery scissors, cut a ¾ in. long slit in the white cotton at the back of each large pocket formed by the stitching (cut shorter slits in the smaller areas of the rose). It is surprisingly easy to cut the sheer fabric, so be very careful.

5 Stuff the pockets of the rose with pink scrim, putting the darker scrim toward the center of the flower and the lighter scrim to the outsides of the petals. Use the eye end of the bodkin to move the threads where you want them, turning the picture over occasionally to check your work. Stuff each pocket so that it is filled but not overstuffed—if they are overfull, the picture will pucker.

6 When all the pockets in the rose are stuffed, sew the slits closed with a few overcast stitches to keep the filling in place.

7 Repeat the stuffing and stitching procedure with the leaves, using dark green scrim for the inside edges of the pockets of the leaves and lighter green for the outside edges.

FINISHING

8 Lay the quilting right side down on a flat surface and place the mounting board on top. Stick the raw edges of the fabrics down onto the board with the tape, stretching the fabric evenly as much as possible to keep it taut.

9 Dismantle the frame and lay the embroidered picture in it in place of the glass; fix the backing panel in place securely with the tape.

The marked fabric is basted to the backing fabric to hold it securely in position.

Right: The lines of the design are stitched along by hand or machine, using pink for the rose and circle and green for the leaves and tendrils.

Below left: The pockets formed by the sides of each leaf are stuffed from the back with scrim.

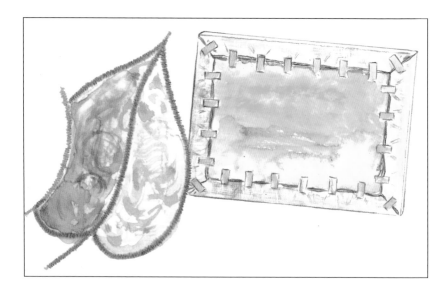

Above right: The quilted picture is stretched and taped over the mounting board before being placed in the picture frame.

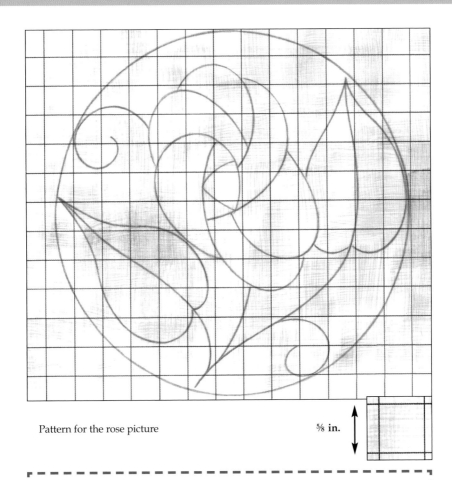

Pattern for the rose picture

⅝ in.

Rainbow Chair Cushion

Trapunto quilting looks very effective when it is combined with contour quilting on a printed fabric. The printed design acts as a stitching guide; then, when the main lines of the design have been stitched, they are stuffed from the back to make the shapes stand out. The cushion in the picture has made the most of a printed rainbow and cloud design, but you could always choose a different fabric. Whichever you choose, pick a design with strong shapes so that the quilting is easy and looks effective. Machine-stitching is quicker for quilting the cushion, but it's possible to quilt by hand if you prefer or want to use a more decorative stitch to outline the shapes.

• QUILTING HANDBOOK •

122

PREPARATION

Wash and press all the fabrics.

Cut the printed fabric and lining to the shape of your chair back, but with a 1 in. margin all around, or enlarge the pattern on the next page and cut it out from your fabrics. Cut a piece the same size and shape from the harmonizing fabric for the back of the cushion cover.

On the right side of the printed fabric, mark a seam allowance of 1 in. along each edge using the water-soluble or fading pen.

QUILTING

1 Lay the lining fabric on a flat surface and the printed fabric right side up on top. Run lines of basting stitches near the main lines of the design to hold the two layers firmly together.

2 Using a straight stitch on the sewing machine or backstitch or chain stitch if you are quilting by hand, stitch around the main shapes on the printed design to form the pockets for stuffing. If one of the shapes goes off the edge of the fabric, complete the pocket by stitching along the seam line.

3 Slit the pockets at the back and stuff the shapes quite firmly with the polyester stuffing. Overcast the slits to close them.

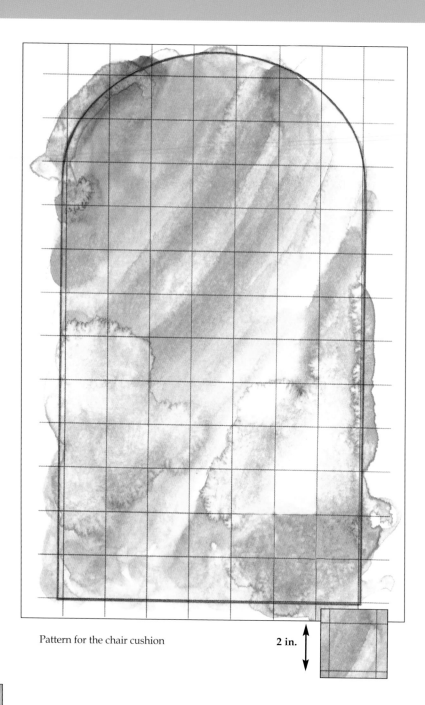

Pattern for the chair cushion

2 in.

FINISHING

4 Cut the strips to fit along each edge of the cushion cover, joining strips where necessary. Join the ends, too, so that you have a complete ring of edging strip ready to go around the quilted fabric.

5 Placing right sides together, pin, baste, and machine-stitch this edging to the quilted fabric along the marked seam line. Press the seam open.

6 Placing right sides together, pin and baste the edging strip to the fabric for the back panel of the cushion cover along the sides and top of the shape, leaving the bottom edge open. Stitch a 1 in. seam and press it open.

7 Turn the cushion cover right side out and insert the piece of foam. Turn under 1 in. on the raw edges and slip-stitch them neatly together to close the gap.

8 Cut the tape into four equal lengths, fold each length in half, and stitch them to the four corners at the back of the cushion along the fold line.

TIPS
FOR PROFESSIONAL RESULTS

• Make sure to buy fire-retardant foam for your cushion (this is available from most home decorating stores).

• Find a place that cuts foam to size and tell them the exact shape that you want; this is easier than trying to cut the foam yourself and produces a neater result.

• If you want a thicker cushion, choose foam 1½ or 2 in. thick and cut your edging strips 2 in. wider than your foam.

• You can add extra decoration to your design by using chain stitch or a fancy machine-stitch for outlining the shape, but make sure that it is a firm stitch that will produce well-defined pockets.

• Couching a thick contrasting thread around the edges of the main shape can look very striking and add extra texture.

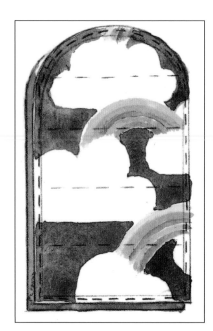

Left: The seam allowance is drawn in on the printed fabric, and this is basted securely to the lining fabric.

Below: The edge of each shape is stitched around; where the shape crosses the seam allowance, the stitching follows the marked line so that there is still a pocket to stuff.

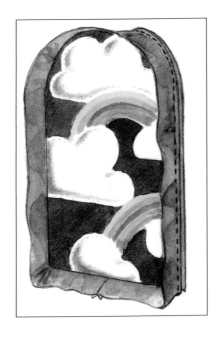

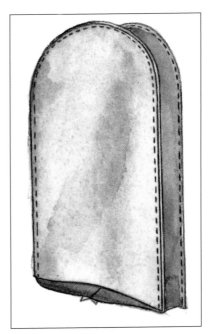

Top left: The edging strips are stitched together to form a continuous loop, then placed on the quilted cushion front with right sides facing. They are then basted in place and machine-stitched along the seam line.

Top right: The back panel has been stitched to the front and lining, and now the cushion cover is slipped over the foam shape and the edges of the opening at the bottom are slip-stitched together.

Right: The four ties are sewn in place on the back of the cushion at each corner.

Chinese Headboard

This project shows how adaptable corded quilting can be. The basic technique is the same as for the previous projects, but has been scaled up and used for a very large design. For this striking geometric pattern, based on a traditional Chinese screen design, the channels for the cord are formed by stitching colored woven tape onto a plain white background. Obviously larger channels need larger cord, so this design makes use of thin synthetic rope. Once the quilting is complete, the design is mounted onto a foam pad to form a comfortable cushion.

MATERIALS

Strong white fabric: 2 pieces,
24 x 56 in.; 2 pieces, 4 x 24 in.; and
2 pieces, 4 x 56 in.

4 strips of blue fabric, 10 x 12 in.

Blue seam binding or similar tape,
1 in. wide and 18 yd. long

Blue and white sewing thread

Synthetic rope, about ⅜ in.
in diameter and 18 yd. long

1 foam pad, 2 in. thick and
measuring 22 x 54 in.

Roll of wallpaper or shelf-lining paper
for enlarging the chart

Black felt-tip pen

Water-soluble or fading pen

PREPARATION

Wash and press fabrics.

Enlarge the design to the correct size and mark the lines with the black felt-tip pen.

Put one of the large pieces of the white fabric over the chart and trace the lines of the design showing through with the water-soluble or fading pen.

QUILTING

1 Lay the marked fabric on a flat surface and pin the blue tape along the lines of the design, cutting it where lines cross. Pleat and tape carefully where it has to turn corners to miter them; where the tape begins and ends on each part of the design, fold the ends under diagonally so that they look like other corners. Where one line runs into another, cut the lower tape slightly longer so that it tucks under the upper tape and will be secured by the top tape's stitching.

2 When all the tapes have been pinned in place, baste them to the backing fabric for extra security.

The design is marked on the right side of the headboard front; make sure that the lines are straight and the corners square.

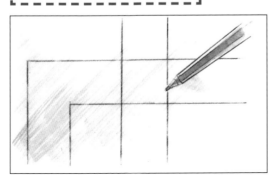

3 Using blue thread, machine-stitch along both edges of each tape. Don't stitch down the diagonal folds on the corners; just stitch down the edges.

4 Secure the corner folds with blue slip stitches worked by hand, making sure that you stitch only through the tape, not into the backing fabric.

5 Following the instructions given on page 58, thread each channel with the synthetic rope (the rope should be thin enough for you to just push it through each channel, as you will not be able to use any kind of bodkin).

FINISHING

6 With right sides together, stitch a 1 in. seam along the long edges of each of the blue fabric strips. Turn them right side out and press. Topstitch in white along both edges of the strips.

7 Fold the strips in half, aligning the raw ends, and topstitch across their width about halfway down (this makes a casing for the inner curtain rod to slip through). Pin the loops in position on the top front of the cushion back and machine-stitch across them, close to the raw edges of the cushion back fabric, several times.

8 With right sides together, stitch the four remaining pieces of white fabric together across their widths in 1 in. seams.

9 With right sides together, pin, baste, and machine-stitch this ring of fabric to the quilted front, matching the seams in the side fabrics to the corners of the front piece, in a 1 in. seam; press the seam open.

10 With right sides together, pin, baste, and machine-stitch the side pieces to the cushion back in a 1 in. seam, leaving one side open. Press the seam open and turn the cover right side out.

11 Insert the foam pad through the opening or turn the raw edges under and insert a zipper.

12 Hang the cushion from a blue or natural wood curtain rod mounted on the wall at the head of the bed so that the cushion hangs at a comfortable height.

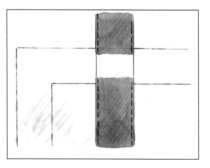

The tape is basted firmly in position along the marked lines.

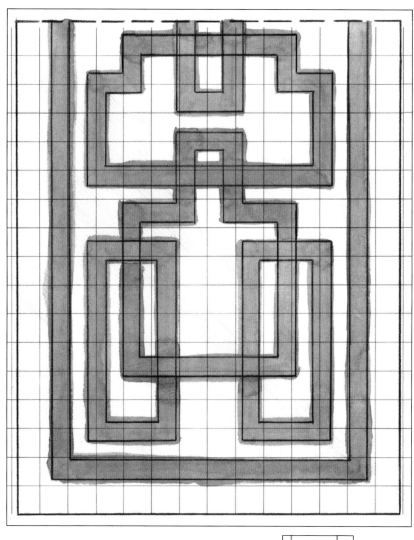

Chart for the headboard

1½ in.

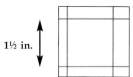

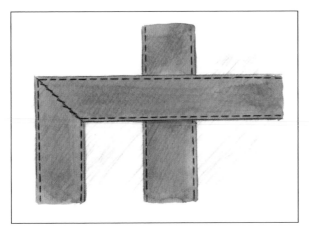

The tapes are stitched in position along both edges and the corner folds are slip-stitched in place—through the tape only, not through the background fabric.

Right: Detail showing the tapes stitched into position.

Below: The blue fabric strips are seamed and topstitched. They are then folded into loops and sewn to the right side of the cushion back at even intervals along the top.

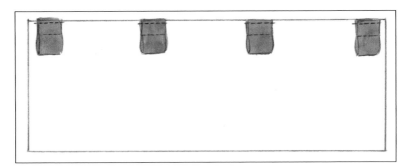

The edge pieces are joined to form a continuous strip, which is basted to the quilted cushion front, matching the corners carefully with the right sides together. The seam is then stitched by machine.

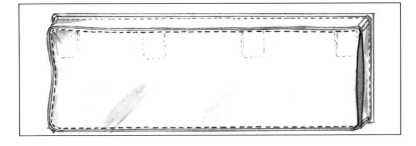

The edge pieces are basted to the cushion back along three sides, then machine-stitched together, with the fourth side left open so that the cover can be turned right side out.

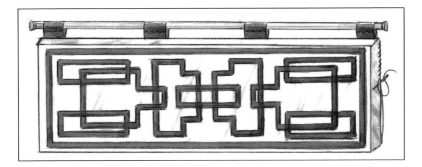

The cushion cover is stuffed with the foam pad and the open edges are then closed with slip stitches, or a zipper is inserted so that the cover can be removed for cleaning.

TIPS
FOR PROFESSIONAL RESULTS

• If you cut a length of thin cardboard the exact width of your tape, you can use this to measure and mark the lines as you trace them onto the white fabric, which will mean that your lines will be straighter than if you trace them all freehand. Some yardsticks are exactly 1 in. wide, so they can be used in the same way.

• Use straight seam binding instead of bias binding for this design, as bias binding will stretch and you will want the tapes to stay as firm as possible.

• If you use nylon rope for the threading tapes, you obviously won't be able to thread it onto any kind of bodkin. To keep the ends from fraying, carefully hold them in a flame for a few seconds. This will bond them and give the rope a harder tip, which will be easier to push through the tapes.

VARIATIONS

Any color of fabric and tape can be used for the headboard design. For a subtle effect, use two shades of one color or appliqué a plain tape to a softly patterned background.

For a double bed, extend some of the horizontal lines of the pattern, but work out the design on a piece of paper before you transfer it to the fabric.

If you have made the headboard, you may want to add some other threaded tape patterns in other parts of your bedroom decor to echo the headboard design. Try making a border at the bottom or down the center seam of plain curtains—perhaps using narrower tape and cord in a reduced-size version of blue-and-white design or one of the alternatives on the opposite page. Or, if you're feeling really creative, you could embroider a rug in large cross-stitch on rug canvas or pick up the design across the top of a comforter cover or bedspread. For a really coordinated look, you might want to try fabric-painting the design on the top edge of a sheet or making it into a repeat pattern to be stenciled around the walls as a frieze.

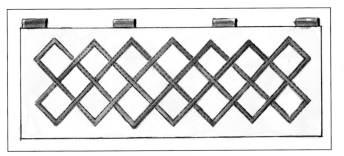

Left: This simple pattern can be extended or reduced to fit a headboard of any size; the color scheme produces a soft, countryside effect, which could be enhanced by appliquéing fabric flowers over the trellis.

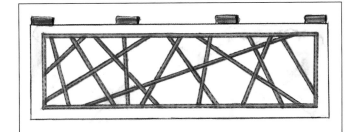

Right: This pretty green-on-green design uses random straight lines interweaving across the shape of the headboard; you don't have to use the arrangement shown here—you can adapt it to the exact dimensions.

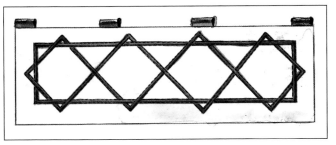

Left: This stark variation on the trellis pattern looks very high-tech: Use it as part of a simple color scheme such as black, white, gray, and red; for a bold look, use a combination of bright primary colors.

Spring Wall Hanging

The beautiful, abstract shape of this quilt is based on the Chinese character for spring, and the subject is reflected in the soft colors used. The piece of silk used for the background is dyed with gentle blends of pinks, mauves, and blues, and then threads in the same color ranges are used for the stitching. The pattern is a simple repeat of equilateral triangles, which are stitched in straight lines across the shape in three directions, and the design is completed with a line of quilting around the edge. Tassels are made from a selection of threads and stitched to the design at intervals.

MATERIALS

1 piece of white silk,
40 in. square

1 piece of white backing fabric, the
same size as the silk fabric

A selection of threads in pinks, blues,
purples, and mauves (use any mixture
of stranded floss, ordinary sewing
threads, pearl cotton, matte
embroidery cotton, threads of different
thicknesses, silks, etc.)

Silk paints in pink and blue

Two lengths of bamboo or dowel to
fit the top and bottom of the
finished hanging

Water-soluble or fading pen

PREPARATION

Press the fabrics.

Enlarge the chart to the correct size onto a large piece of paper.

In a selection of paper cups, mix up several diluted colors in the pink, blue, and mauve range (make mauves by mixing some pinks and blues in different amounts).

Lay sheets of plain paper on a flat surface and lay the silk on top. Wet the fabric thoroughly by spraying it with water.

Using a wide brush, paint the diluted silk paints onto the fabric; where two colors meet, brush that area with extra water to make the shades run into each other. Leave the edges of the fabric unpainted, fading the colors out gently as you move toward the edges.

Leave the silk out to dry completely.

Lay the silk out on a flat surface, right side up, and transfer the spring design to it using a water-soluble or fading pen.

Left: Close detail
of the stitches on
the wall hanging.

Using the same pen, draw a series of parallel lines straight across the shape, from side to side, with exactly 1 in. gaps between each line. Draw the lines only within the outlines of the spring design.

Choose any point along one of these lines near the center of the shape and draw a diagonal line at sixty degrees from the horizontal. Draw another series of lines parallel to this one, again making them exactly 1 in. apart.

You should now be able to join up the intersections on the lines with a third series of parallel lines at the opposite angle, producing a grid of equilateral triangles.

QUILTING

1 Lay the backing fabric right side down on a flat surface and position the silk on top, right side up. Baste the two layers together with lines of basting stitches around the outside of the marked shape.

2 Using the various threads, stitch along the straight lines and the outline of a shape, using running stitches and making the stitches on the top of the fabric twice as long as the stitches on the back.

FINISHING

3 Make small tassels by winding loops of mixed threads around several fingers. Slip the loops off and wind the thread around a short way in from the top and bottom. Cut the loops across the center, producing two tassels. Make several more and sew them on at different points around the edges of the design.

4 Fold under a double hem to the wrong side at each side of the wall hanging and stitch it down by machine or by hand.

5 Fold under a small turning to the wrong side at the top and bottom of the hanging, then fold under again by about 1½ in. and stitch along the edge of the first fold to make casings for the bamboo or dowel.

6 Sew two fabric loops or curtain rings, or work buttonhole stitch loops, on the back of the casing where they are hidden from view; use these to hang up the embroidery. Alternatively, make a cord by twisting together some of the threads you have used for quilting and attach it to each end of the top rod.

A

TIPS
FOR PROFESSIONAL RESULTS

• If you don't feel confident about painting your silk, work the design on a solid color or choose an iridescent silk, which incorporates different shades.

• Put lots of variety and texture into the stitching by using two different threads in the needle at once — for example, two colors of stranded floss or a pale matte cotton with a strand of darker silk, or a matte thread together with a strand of metallic thread.

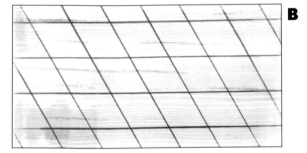

A Opposite page: A series of parallel lines is drawn at even intervals across the spring design using the water-soluble or fading pen.

B Above: Another series of parallel lines is drawn at sixty degrees to the first ones, making sure that they are spaced evenly.

C Below: The intersections between these lines are joined with diagonal lines to produce a grid of equilateral triangles.

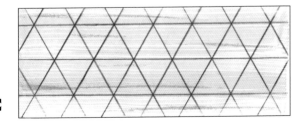

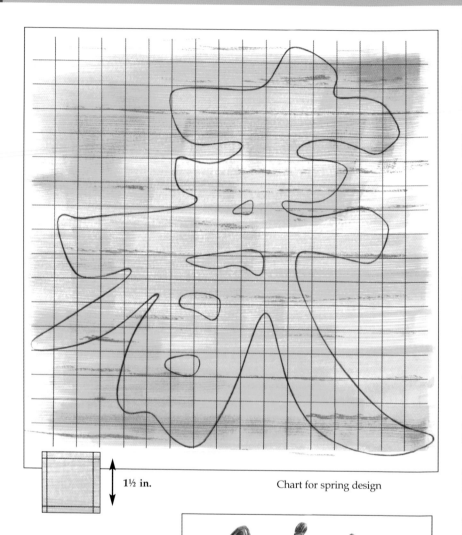

1½ in.

Chart for spring design

Loops of mixed threads are
bound at the top and bottom,
then cut across the middle to
produce two tassels to decorate
the edges of the design.

Nightgown Case

This project — a pretty way to keep your nightgown handy for bedtime — makes use of the technique known as appliqué perse, which involves applying shapes cut from printed fabric to the background. It's a very good technique to start with if you are new to appliqué, as you don't have to worry about transferring the lines of a design; you simply choose your shapes from those available in your print. To keep things simple, the quilting is done at the same time as appliqué. The stitching is done by machine zigzag, as you need a thick band of stitching to conceal the raw edges.

PREPARATION

Wash and press the satin and
printed fabrics.

Enlarge the pattern pieces to
the correct size onto paper and
cut them out.

Cut one of the square shapes
and two of the rectangular shapes
out of the satin. Cut one square
shape from the muslin and one
from the batting.

QUILTING

1 Choose the part of the printed
pattern on the fabric that you
want to use on the nightgown
case and cut it out, leaving a
½–¾ in. margin all around.

2 Iron transfer fusing web
onto the back of the shape.

3 Using the embroidery
scissors, cut around the motif,
leaving a margin of about ¹⁄₁₆ in.
all around the edges.

4 Peel off the backing paper
and position the motif on
the front of the satin square.
When you are happy with the
positioning, iron the motif onto
the satin to bond it in place.

Left: An attractively shaped motif is
cut from the printed fabric, leaving a
generous margin around the edges.

5 Place the muslin on a flat surface and put the batting on top. Lay the satin square, right side up, on top of the batting and baste all three layers together around the edges of the motif, adding extra lines of basting if the fabrics need it.

6 Using close zigzag or satin stitch, stitch around the edges of the main lines of the motif, matching the colors of the threads to the colors on the printed fabric.

7 Remove the basting threads and press the design gently on the wrong side.

FINISHING

8 Press under and stitch a double hem along the long straight edges of the satin rectangles.

9 If you are cording the edges, cut bias strips from the extra satin, join them, and baste them over the cord.

10 Lay the quilted square right side up on a flat surface and position the rectangles facedown over the top so that the hemmed edges overlap down the middle. (If you are using cording, insert it between the layers around the outside edges at this stage.) Pin and baste around the edges for a ¼ in. seam and machine-stitch along this line twice for strength.

11 Turn the nightgown case right side out and press it gently.

Left: Transfer fusing web is ironed onto the back of the fabric shape, then the edges of the fabric are trimmed close to the outline of the motif.

Right: The backing paper is peeled away from the back of the motif.

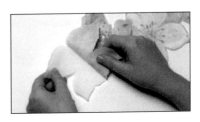

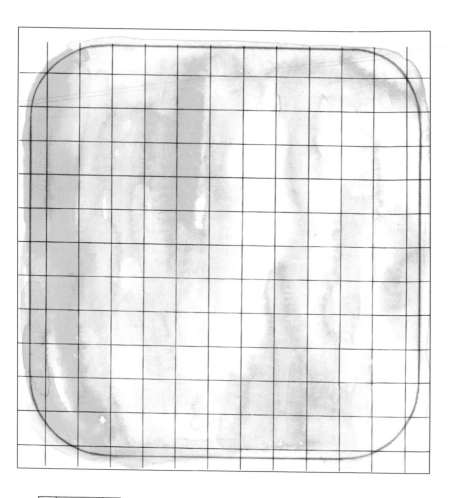

1¼ in.

Pattern for nightgown case front

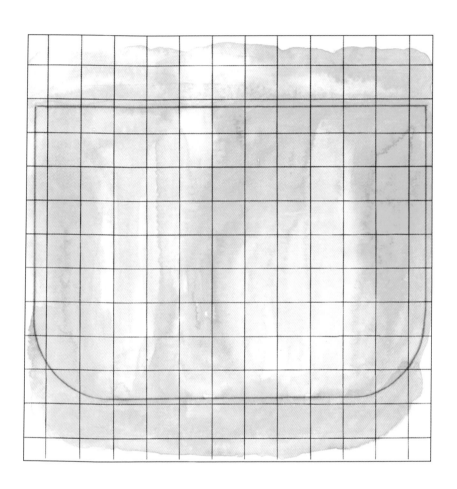

Pattern for nightgown case back

1¼ in.

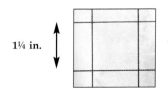

VARIATIONS

Simply choosing a different color for the satin background creates quite a different effect, as does a bright, firm cotton.

The same pattern can be used to make a square cushion cover — simply cut the pattern shapes with square corners instead of rounded ones and put a pillow form of the appropriate size inside when stitching has been completed. You don't have to use one large motif for the design on the front, either. You can cut

The motif is positioned on the front of the satin square and ironed in place.

The satin square, batting, and muslin are basted together around the motif, then the main outlines of the motif are stitched over with machine zigzag or satin stitch in the matching colors.

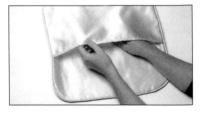

The front, backing pieces, and cording are stitched together in one seam and then the nightgown case is turned right side out.

smaller ones and scatter them over the front of the satin.

Bright Rug

Even large shapes can be decorated with quilting and appliqué, as this rug shows. The bright primary colors against the white background give it a very "modern art" look. The appliqué itself is straightforward, but the secret of success lies in the accurate cutting and positioning of the colored pieces on the background, which is helped by using transfer fusing web. Choose a durable upholstery fabric for the background so that it will stand up to wear and tear, and when the rug becomes grubby, it can be easily washed in a washing machine using the delicate cycle.

MATERIALS

2 pieces of strong white fabric, each 40 x 50 in.

1 piece of extrathick batting, the same size as the white fabric

1 piece of yellow fabric, 39 x 43–44 in.

1 piece of blue fabric, (20–30 x 43–44 in.)

1 piece of red fabric, the same size as the blue fabric

2 spools each of machine embroidery thread in blue, red, and yellow

White sewing thread

Transfer fusing web—about 2 sq. yd.

PREPARATION

Wash and press all the fabrics (check that all the colored fabrics are colorfast).

On the paper side of the fusing web, draw eighteen boxes—each 7½ in. square—and cut them out.

Draw wiggly lines in pencil to separate each square into three areas. You don't need to be too careful with the lines—let them flow freely—but remember that the shapes will be reversed when they are cut out of the fabric.

Arrange the fusing web squares in the pattern shown in the rug chart, altering the order they are in until you are happy with the balance of the design. Then mark each square with a number (1 to 18) to designate its position in the layout.

On the back of the squares, mark each separate section with a

Detail of bright rug

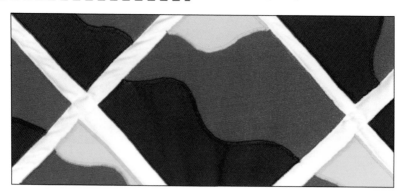

Pattern for bright rug

number and a letter to denote the square it belongs to and the color fabric you will use for it. So, for example, square 1 will be divided into three sections: 1Y for the piece that will be yellow, 1R for the piece that will be red, 1B for the piece that will be blue, and so on. Work down from yellow through red to blue, on each square.

Cut along the wiggly lines to separate the pieces, then group them into three piles by their color codes.

Iron all the yellow pieces onto the back of the yellow fabric and repeat the process with the red pieces and fabric and the blue pieces and fabric. Cut out the fabric pieces, but don't peel off the paper.

Reassemble the squares on the background fabric in the original order. You should now have eighteen squares, each made up from a yellow section, a red section, and a blue section, arranged evenly on your background fabric.

Working on one square at a time, peel off the backing papers and carefully reposition the pieces on the background, abutting their edges. Iron them to bond them to the background fabric. Repeat the process until all the shapes are fused in place.

QUILTING

1 Thread your machine with one color and use a wide satin stitch or close zigzag to stitch around all the fabric sections in that color. Repeat with the two remaining colors. When the stitching is complete, press the work thoroughly.

2 Lay the other piece of white fabric on a flat surface and lay the batting on top of it. Position the appliquéd fabric on top of the batting and secure all the layers together with regular lines of basting stitches, crisscrossing between the diamonds.

3 Set your machine to a long straight stitch ⅛ in., thread it with the white thread, and stitch across the quilt so that the lines of stitching run close to each edge of each diamond. Continue the lines of stitching out to the edges of the fabric.

4 Remove the basting threads.

FINISHING

5 Cut 4 in. strips of the remaining yellow fabric to fit the sides and ends of the rug, with 1 in. extra at each end (join the fabric to form the strips if necessary).

6 Cut some strips of the remaining blue and red fabric to the same width and back them with transfer using web.

7 Cut the red and blue strips into random lengths with wiggly lines and position them in a pleasing arrangement on the yellow strips. Keep the fabric colors in the same sequence all the way around, and use the red or blue fabric to cover any seams in the yellow strips. Peel off the backing papers and then iron the pieces to bond them firmly to the yellow fabric.

8 Stitch along the wavy lines in the appropriate-colored thread, using satin or close zigzag stitching.

9 Use the decorated strips to bind the edges of the rug. The machine-stitching creates a quilted border around the edges of the rug.

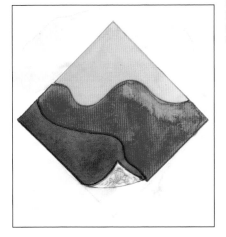

Having been backed with fusing web, the fabric pieces are laid on the background fabric in their squares, with the edges of the pieces abutting; they are then ironed in place.

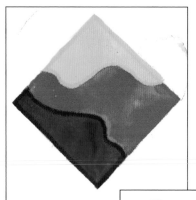

The raw edges of the shapes are stitched along in satin or close zigzag stitching using threads matching the colors.

The quilted fabric, batting, and backing fabric are basted together, then quilted by machine in long, straight lines of stitching worked diagonally across the rug, using the edges of the squares as stitching guides.

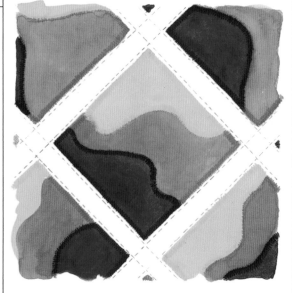

Random shapes of red and blue fabric are applied to the yellow edging strips, again being stitched with thread of a matching color.

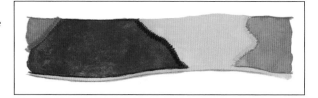

Quilted Play Mat

Every child loves a special place to play with their toys, and this play mat is ideal. The design includes roads, railroads, paths, water, and favorite items such as a bandstand and an ice-cream stand, so there's plenty of opportunity for varied play. Use as many different fabrics for the appliqué as possible so that you have a range of textures and colors. This is an excellent way to use up all those scraps of fabric in your sewing chest, for almost no scrap is too small to be incorporated somewhere in the design. Each fabric piece is backed with transfer fusing web, then the appliqué and quilting are done together by machine.

MATERIALS

1 piece of light green cotton or polyester-cotton fabric, 39 in. square

1 piece of white fabric, the same size as the green fabric

2 layers of thick batting, the same size as the green fabric

4 strips of blue fabric, each 6 in. wide and 39 in. long

Large scraps of beige, pale blue, gray, and medium-green fabric

Lots of small scraps of fabrics in bright colors, solid and printed

Transfer fusing web, about ½–1 sq. yd.

Sewing thread in a neutral color

PREPARATION

Wash and press the green and white fabrics and other cotton scraps that you intend to use.

Tape together several large pieces of paper and enlarge the play mat design to the correct size.

On the front of the fusing web, trace the shapes required for the paths across the park. Cut the shapes out, iron them onto the back of the beige fabric, and cut around the shapes.

Peel off the backing paper, position the pieces of beige fabric on the right side of the green fabric, and iron to bond them in place.

Repeat these last two steps with the shapes and fabrics for the pond, the hedges, and the road.

Gradually work through all the medium-size elements of the design, positioning the larger ones (such as the bandstand roof) first, then the smaller ones, and iron them all into place.

Finish with the smallest pieces of fabric, such as the deck chair struts and the railroad ties.

Detail of the quilted play mat

QUILTING

1 Lay the white backing fabric on a flat surface and put the layers of batting on top, smoothing them out. Lay the fabric with the appliquéd picture on it, right side up, on top of the batting. Baste through all four layers at regular intervals in order to hold them together so that they are flat.

2 Set the machine to zigzag and use the same color thread to quilt around each of the pieces. Vary the size of the stitches a little to suit the size of the piece you are appliquéing. Begin quilting from the center outward, stitching all the large areas first, then, starting at the center again, stitch around all the small areas. Lines such as the railroad tracks can be made from lines of zigzag or satin stitch in an appropriate thread color.

3 When stitching is complete, remove the basting threads.

A The largest shapes, such as the pathways, are backed with transfer fusing web, then ironed in place on the background fabric before the other pieces.

B Medium-size pieces, such as the deck chairs and the bandstand, follow next, using exactly the same technique.

C Finally, the smallest details, such as the deck chair struts and the railroad ties, are added to the design and ironed in place.

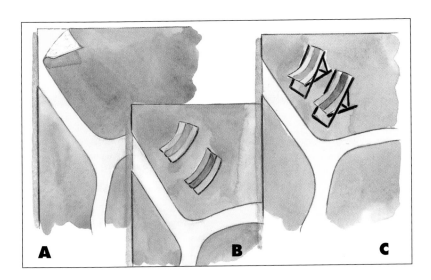

TIPS
FOR PROFESSIONAL RESULTS

• Very tiny bits of fabric tend to fall off while larger pieces are being quilted, so you may find it useful to secure them to the background with a single stitch while you are working on other areas.

• Quilting the small, shaped areas, such as the flowers, can be a bit tricky, so turn the machine speed to slow and manipulate the fabric carefully so that you stitch smoothly around the edges.

• Finish off each line of stitching by pulling the threads through to the back and knotting them; this gives a neater finish on the right side than reversing over the ends.

Once all the fabric pieces are securely in place, the raw edges are stitched along with machine zigzag stitching—one color of thread being used for most of the shapes.

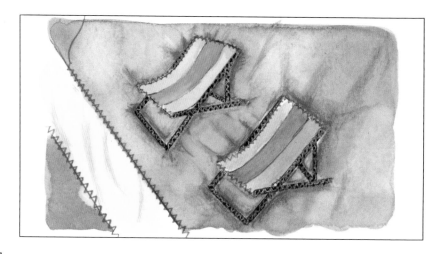

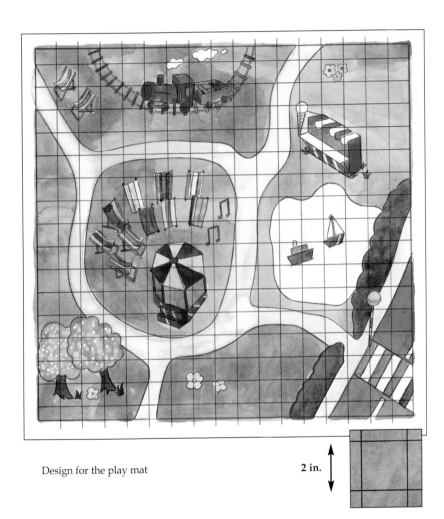

Design for the play mat

2 in.

FINISHING

4 Trim the edges of the play mat by about 1 in. on all sides. Bind the edges of the quilt with the strips of blue fabric, attaching the top and bottom pieces first, then the two side pieces.

Stained Glass Quilt

The spectacular colors and lines of modern stained glass inspired this design, which works its way through a rainbow selection of solid-colored and printed fabrics. The technique used is sometimes also known as stained glass patchwork, but it is actually an appliqué technique. The lines made by the strips of black bias binding imitate the leading stained glass windows. Using bias binding makes it possible to curve the lines easily to follow the bright shapes underneath.

MATERIALS

2 pieces of white cotton or polyester-cotton sheeting, each 60 x 90 in.

1 piece of lightweight polyester batting, the same size as the sheeting

Mixed solid and printed fabrics in bright colors — you will need about 6 sq. yd.

Black bias binding, 1 in. wide and about 55 yd. long

Black bias binding, 2 in. wide and 10 yd. long

2 spools black machine embroidery thread, or similar

Thick black felt-tip pen

Soft pencil or tailor's chalk

PREPARATION

Wash and press all the fabrics you are going to use.

Tape together several large sheets of paper (brown paper or newspaper will do, but white is easier to use) to cover the area of one piece of the sheeting. Divide this area into 10 in. squares with pencil lines and enlarge the chart onto it. Go over all the curves of the quilt design with the thick black felt-tip pen.

Place the chart flat on the floor and tape one of the pieces of sheeting over it. Trace over the curved lines from the chart using either the soft pencil or tailor's chalk (all these lines will be covered by fabric and tape, so don't worry about them showing through).

Mark clearly on the chart which pieces you want in which colors. You can either work through the rainbow, with patterned fabrics down the center as in the photograph on the

Detail of the stained glass quilt

opposite page, or position the colors at random.

Starting at the top of the chart, cut out several pieces and use them as templates for cutting the appropriate fabrics. Position these fabrics within the lines on the marked piece of sheeting. (It is best to do just a few pieces at a time, otherwise you will soon lose track of which piece goes where.)

When you have cut and positioned all the fabric pieces, check that you are happy with the pattern made by the colors. If you are not and there are any you want to change, recut them in different fabrics now.

QUILTING

1 When your design is complete, pin each piece of fabric in position and then carefully and loosely roll up the sheeting. Lay out the other piece of sheeting, position the batting on top, then gently unroll the pinned design over the batting.

2 Check that all the edges of the layers are even, then baste all three layers together with regular rows of basting across the middle of the quilt.

3 Cut appropriate lengths of the narrow bias binding and position them, one at a time, over where the fabric pieces join, straddling the pieces of fabric

evenly. Curve the binding gently to follow the curve of the marked line. Pin and baste each piece of binding down both edges so that the raw edges of fabric are firmly trapped. Continue until all the black tapes are in position.

4 Thread your sewing machine with the black thread and set it to a medium-length straight stitch (about ⅛ in.). Machine-stitch along both edges of each strip of bias binding, stitching the inside of each curve first. With this method the quilting and appliqué are thus done simultaneously. Where one bias strip crosses another, simply stitch across the joint.

5 Remove all the basting threads once all the tape has been stitched down.

FINISHING

6 Bind the edges of the quilt with the wide bias binding.

VARIATIONS

Many different solid-colored or printed fabrics can be used to stunning effect with this technique. Instead of using bright cotton fabrics, you can substitute pastels or shades of just a few colors, or even satins or metallic fabrics. The leading doesn't have to be black—you might choose instead to pick out one of the colors from your other fabrics.

90 in.

60 in.

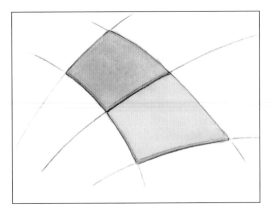

The pattern pieces are cut out of the different fabrics, using the enlarged chart as a cutting guide, then laid into position within the lines marked on the background fabric.

Once all the fabric pieces are in position and the quilt top has been basted to the batting, the black bias binding is pinned along the lines where the fabric pieces meet, the joint running down the center of the bias binding strips.

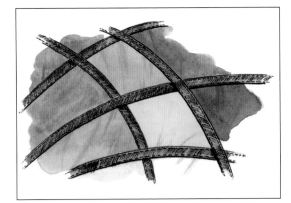

Using machine straight stitch, both edges of the bias binding are stitched down, trapping the raw edges of the fabric pieces underneath them and quilting at the same time.

Above: Glitter is the watchword for this example, and in total contrast, the example below captures an English country cottage style. The two samples of stained glass appliqué shown here demonstrate just how different a pattern can look depending on the fabrics used. The exact same pattern has been used for cutting the fabric pieces and positioning the bias binding.

TIPS
FOR PROFESSIONAL RESULTS

• Buy a "bed-size" piece of batting so that you don't have to join two or more widths.

• For the sake of economy, contact a wholesale supplier, and see if you can buy the bias binding you need wholesale, or make your own bias strips from black fabric.

• Make sure that you stitch the inside edge of each curve before the outside edge, as this prevents the binding from stretching too much as it is stitched.

• Adjoining pieces of the same color can be cut together as one piece of fabric—you don't need to cut down the line between them.

• When you come to stitching the black tapes near the center of the design, roll the tapes near the right-hand side of the quilt up tightly so that it will fit under the arm of the sewing machine.

Christmas Tree

The traditional Christmas tree is interpreted here in a padded patchwork shape for this hanging Christmas decoration. Choose as many different Christmassy fabrics as possible (many quilting retailers sell packs containing small pieces of suitable fabrics) or choose solids and prints in combinations of red, green, and white. The pattern is very easy and makes a good project for newcomers to patchwork. The triangles are pieced by hand or machine before being quilted.

MATERIALS

19 different scraps of cotton or polyester-cotton fabrics in Christmassy colors and/or patterns

Blue or green satin ribbon, 20 in., tied into a bow

Green bias binding, 1 in. wide and 2 yd. long

Piece of thick batting, 20 in. square

Piece of solid red and green backing fabric, the same size as the batting

Red sewing thread

Piece of cardboard large enough to trace triangle onto (see template on next page)

Soft pencil

PREPARATION

Trace the triangle onto a piece of cardboard and cut out carefully. This is your template for the patchwork pieces.

Press all the fabrics that you will be using.

Draw around the template on the back of each fabric scrap using a soft pencil. Cut out the shapes, leaving a ¾ in. seam allowance all around the pencil lines.

Arrange the fabric triangles in a pleasing pattern, following the shape of the Christmas tree in the picture on page 164.

Stitch the triangles into rows across the shape; first pin and baste each seam together, then stitch by hand or machine along the pencil lines. Press each seam open before you stitch the next.

Trim off any excess fabric from the edges of the seams (but not too close to the seams themselves), and stitch the rows together to form the tree shape. Press the seams open and trim at the edges of the tree shape.

QUILTING

1 Cut the batting and the backing fabric to the shape of the pieced tree.

2 Lay the backing fabric right side down on a flat surface and put the batting on top. Place the pieced tree, right side up,

over the batting and baste all three layers together with several rows of basting stitches.

3 If you are quilting by machine, set your sewing machine to a medium-length straight stitch (1/16 in.) and use the red thread to stitch along the lines of the seams to quilt the shape.

If you are quilting by hand, use the red thread and quilt along the seam lines using running stitch or backstitch.

FINISHING

4 Edge the shape with the green bias binding and sew the bow in place at the top of the "pot."

5 Sew small loops onto the back of the decoration, or just one at the top so that it can be hung up.

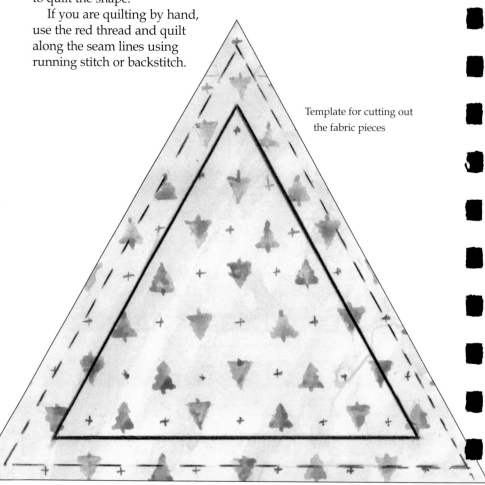

Template for cutting out
the fabric pieces

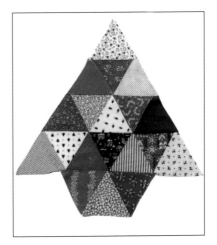

The triangles are marked on the back of the fabrics and cut out, adding a seam allowance all around, then laid out to form a pleasing effect.

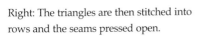

Right: The triangles are then stitched into rows and the seams pressed open.

Left: The rows of triangles are stitched to each other to produce a tree shape, with the seam lines matched carefully, then the seams are pressed open.

Right: The batting and backing fabric are cut into shape, then basted together with the patchwork shape on top. Each seam line is quilted with a straight line of red machine stitching.

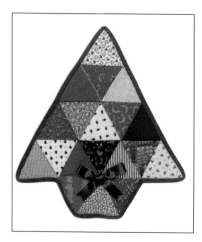

The finished Christmas tree

Striped Jerkin

The bright jerkin shown here makes use of a variation of the technique known as "quilt as you go." The seams that join the strips of colored fabric quilt the garment at the same time. This is an ideal project for using up small scraps of fabric, making them into a garment that will delight a young child, but be sure to choose fabrics that are of similar weights and fibers. The pattern given here fits a child aged about six, but you could scale it up or down slightly for a younger or older child. Seams are kept to a minimum and the edges are finished with bias binding in a selection of colors that harmonize well with stripes. Make the jerkin extra useful by choosing colors that match outfits already in the child's wardrobe.

PREPARATION

Enlarge the jerkin pattern to the correct size and cut the shape out of paper.

Wash and press all the fabrics you will be using.

Fold the white fabric in half across its width, place the "fold" edge of the pattern along the fold, and cut out the fabric to produce the jerkin shape. Do the same with the muslin and batting.

Place the muslin shape on a flat surface and position the batting on top. Baste the two pieces together with lines of close basting stitches across the shapes and around the edges.

QUILTING

1 Choose a color for your first strip and cut the fabric to the desired width, adding a ¼ in. seam allowance along one of the long edges. With the batting faceup, baste the fabric strip, right side up, along the far left side of the jerkin shape and trim it so that it follows the curve.

2 Choose a fabric for your next strip and cut it to the desired width, adding ¼ in. at both sides for seams. Place it right side down over the first strip, lining up the right-hand edges, and baste down ¼ in. from the edges. Stitch along this line in machine straight stitch, or in close running stitches if sewing by hand.

3 Fold the strip over to the right so that it is now right side up, and trim the top and bottom to the shape of the batting and muslin if necessary.

4 Continue in the same way across the jerkin shape, varying the colors and widths of the strips to make an attractive design. Make sure that you keep each strip vertical.

5 When you have completed the final strip, fold it over to the right, as before, and baste it down. Stitch around all the raw edges of the jerkin shape, very close to the edge, with a line of straight machine stitching.

FINISHING

6 With right sides together, join the shoulder seams of the jerkin, taking a very narrow seam allowance.

7 Stitch the shoulder seams of the lining fabric in the same way.

8 With wrong sides together, baste the lining inside the jerkin shape 1 in. from the raw edges.

9 Bind the armholes and the other raw edges of the jerkin with the bias binding.

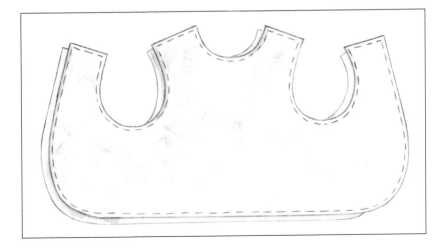

The lining, batting, and muslin are cut into shape, and the batting is then basted to the muslin in order to hold the two layers together during quilting.

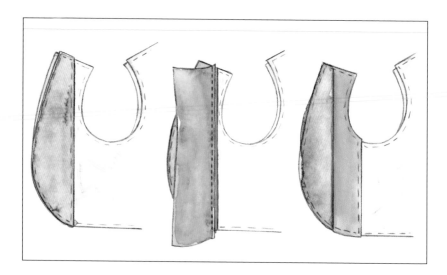

The first strip of fabric is cut to the required width, then basted, right side up, to the left-hand edge of the jerkin shape. It is then trimmed to fit.

The next strip of fabric is cut to the required width and placed facedown over the first strip, and the right-hand edges are stitched down.

The new strip of fabric is folded over to the right, basted in place, and then trimmed to shape along the top and bottom.

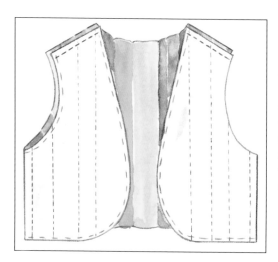

When the patchwork is complete, a line of stitching is worked along all the raw edges to hold the layers together firmly. The jerkin shape is folded, with the right sides together, and the shoulders are joined in a narrow seam.

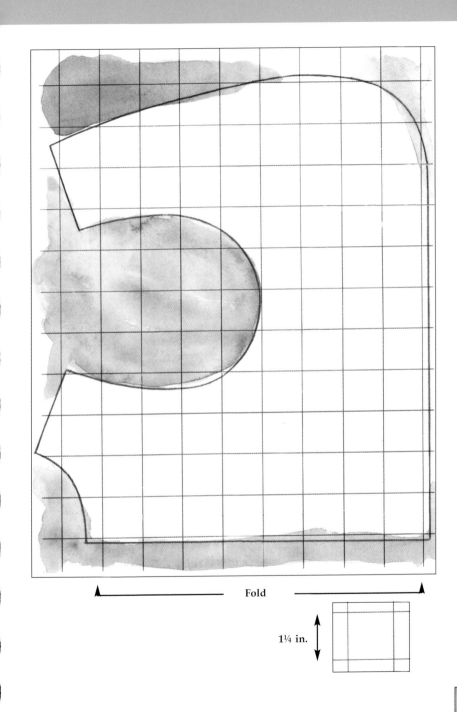

Fold

1¼ in.

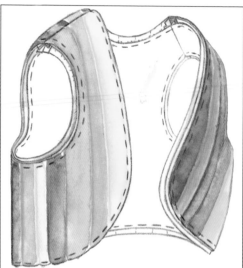

Left: The shoulder seams of the lining are joined in the same way and the lining is basted inside the patchwork, wrong sides together.

Below: The raw edges are bound with bias binding in three different colors.

TIPS
FOR PROFESSIONAL RESULTS

• If you aren't confident about stitching your seams straight, mark the seam allowances on the edges of the fabric strips in soft pencil or tailor's chalk.

• If the weave in your fabric is straight, you can produce straight strips by making a small nick in the edge of each fabric and tearing it down the grain.

VARIATIONS

Choose solid-colored fabrics in a range of pastel shades if you want a more subtle effect, or select harmonizing prints and solid colors.

If you prefer, you can finish the edges in the same color of bias binding instead of using three different colors.

For a special occasion, such as a party or a wedding, you could make a jerkin for a little girl in pastel satins or pinwale corduroy—perhaps to match a party dress.

Pencil or Sewing Kit Case

This case is ideal for storing pencils or carrying your sewing kit to classes or on trips. Make it in these bright colors or devise your own color scheme. The finished size is approximately 11 x 7 in.

MATERIALS

Cotton dress-weight fabric, in the
following colors:
Green, red, and purple: one piece of
each color, 12 x 4 in.;
Yellow, ¼ yd.;
14 squares in plain colors,
each 3¼ in. square

10 in. zipper

PREPARATION

All measurements include a ¼ in.
seam allowance.

From the green, red, and
purple, cut two pieces, each
2 in. x 12 in. From the yellow,
cut two pieces, each 12 in. x 8 in.

Make the points by folding
the small squares of the fabric
diagonally across once, press
with a hot iron, then diagonally
across again so that you have a
folded triangle with all raw
edges together.

TIPS
FOR MAKING THE TRIANGLE POINTS

• Cut the squares.

• Fold diagonally and press.

• Fold again; all raw edges are
now together.

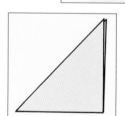

QUILTING

1 Mark the center point of each strip. Take a green strip and position two triangles on top, all raw edges together, and pin on the triangles. Then place the red strip on top, right side down, pin and stitch, taking a ¼ in. seam allowance and trapping the triangle edges in the seam.

2 Fold the red strip upward, pin three triangles along the top edge, then place and pin the purple strip on top and stitch as before.

3 Fold the purple strip upward and pin two more triangles along the top edge.

4 Take the large yellow rectangle that will form the top strip and the lining. Pin it to the purple strip, trapping the triangles as before, and stitch.

5 On the wrong sides, press all the seams toward the yellow piece, then fold this over, placing the raw edges together. Press firmly and topstitch just above the seams through all the layers. Repeat for the other side of the case.

FINISHING

6 Lay the two sides on a flat surface, right sides up, folded edges together, and insert the zipper in the center. Stitch in using a zipper foot.

7 Fold the case right sides together, pin and stitch down the sides through four thicknesses and along the bottom, being careful not to trap the points in the seam.

8 Trim seams and zigzag-stitch to neaten the inside. Turn right side out and press.

Pin two triangles to the bottom strip.

center

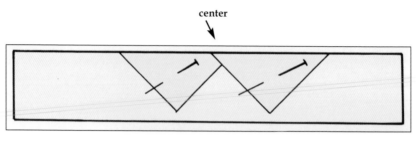

To add a second strip, sew on the second strip, trapping the triangle points in the seam.

Lay another strip on top. Stitch the two strips together, trapping triangles in the seam.

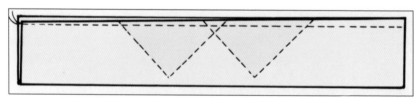

Fold.

Topstitch close to seam through all thicknesses.

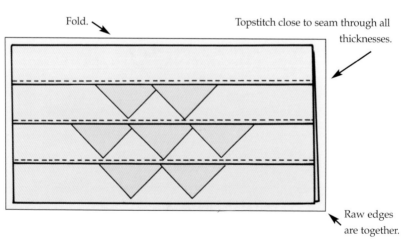

Raw edges are together.

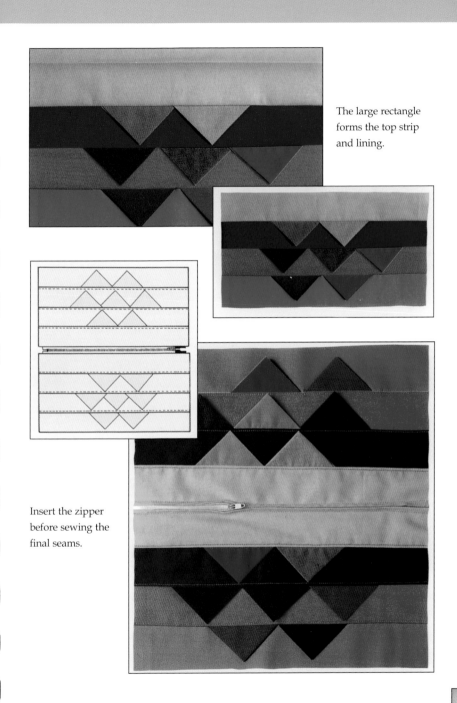

The large rectangle forms the top strip and lining.

Insert the zipper before sewing the final seams.

Card Trick Shoulder Bag

This simple shoulder bag uses the Card Trick pattern, which gives an intriguing optical illusion of shapes folded over each other. Only two templates are needed: a large and a small half-square triangle. The finished block size is 12 x 12 in.

MATERIALS

Based on 44 in. fabric:

Small pieces in three contrasting fabrics

2 oz. batting, 14 x 28 in.

Lining, ½ yd.

Binding and straps, ¼ yd.

PREPARATION

Draw the block full-size (see next page) and make templates. Make one large triangle A and one small triangle B.

From the large triangle A, cut four of each of the three colors (twelve triangles). From the small triangle B, cut four of each color (twelve triangles).

QUILTING

1 Arrange the patches on a flat surface. Join the small triangles, then make up the squares with the large triangles.

2 Make the center square with four small triangles and the corner squares with eight large triangles (as shown on page 183). Join the squares into strips and finally join these to make the block. Make two blocks.

3 Cut pieces of lining and batting slightly larger than the block and sandwich the batting between the patchwork and the lining. Pin the three layers together and baste in a grid about 4 in. apart.

4 Baste around the outer edge.

5 Quilt by hand or machine around the main shapes ¼ in. from the seams.

6 Trim the lining and batting to the size of the block.

FINISHING

7 Cut three pieces of binding, 2½ in., fold in half lengthwise (wrong sides together), and press.

8 Take a length of binding and place the raw edges against one side (the top) of the block on the back and stitch down through all thicknesses. Repeat with the other block. These bound edges will form the open, top edges of the bag.

9 Now baste the two bottom edges of the blocks together, and using the third piece of binding, repeat, fastening the two blocks together at the bottom edge. Trim the binding to the edges of the blocks and baste the bag together at the two side edges.

10 Cut two more pieces of binding, 2½ x 36 in., fold in half lengthwise, and press as before. Neaten both ends by turning the raw edges in.

11 Bind the edges of the bag together, extending the stitching along the binding to form straps. Knot the two ends together to adjust length.

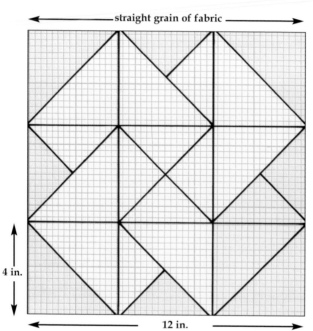

straight grain of fabric →

4 in.

12 in.

Above: The block showing templates and seams

Right: The arrangement of colors in the block

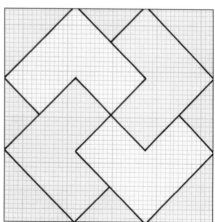

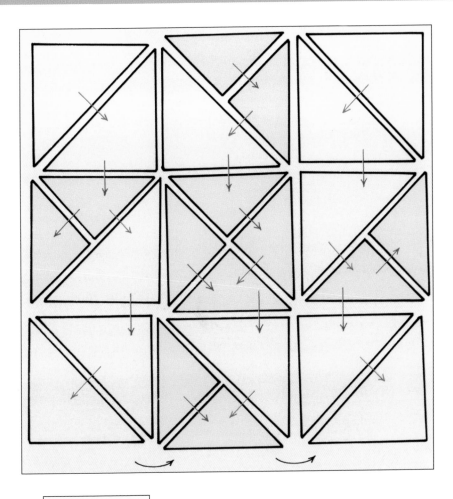

Above: Construction block for Card Trick Shoulder Bag. Assemble each square from the triangles. Sew the squares together in rows, then join the rows to form one block.

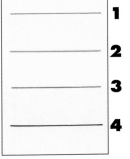

Wave Pillow

A combination of pin tucks and folded strips that can lift away from the background give this pillow an extra dimension. The finished size is 18 x 18 in.

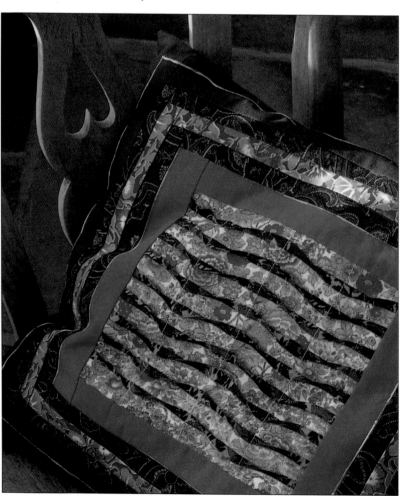

PREPARATION

All measurements include a ¼ in. seam allowance.

From two contrasting fabrics cut ten lighter strips, 1⅛ x 8 in. Fold the darker strips in half lengthwise (wrong sides together) and press. Place folded dark strip against the right side of one of the light ones, raw edges together, and pin another light strip on top.

QUILTING

1 Stitch the two light strips together, trapping the folded strip in the seam and taking just a ¼ in. seam allowance.

2 Continue adding the light strips and trapping the folded dark strips in the seams until you have stitched together all the strips. On the back, press all the seams one way, and on the front, press all the tucks one way. Trim the panel to 7½ in. at the sides.

3 Draw a vertical line down the center of the panel and stitch the tucks down against the light strips. Then press the tucks the other way, i.e., upward, on both sides of the line.

4 Draw two more lines halfway between the center line and the edges of the panel and stitch again, fastening the tucks down the other way. Now press the tucks back in the opposite direction on either side of these two lines of stitching and fasten them down close to the edges.

5 Place the wave panel in the center of the 18 in. backing square, then pin. Using the third fabric, cut two strips of 2 x 7½ in. Place these right side down against the top and bottom of the panel, raw edges together, and stitch through all layers, taking a ¼ in. seam allowance. Turn these strips over and press

TIPS
FOR MAKING THE PIN TUCKS

- Place raw edges together.
- Stitch seam, trapping folded strip.
- A line of stitching is sewn down the center and then the tucks are pressed upward.

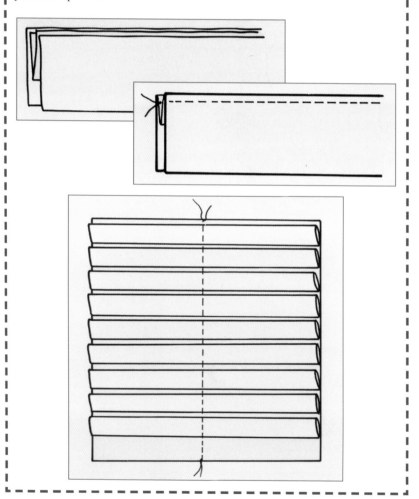

flat against the backing. Now cut two more strips in the same fabric, 2 x 10½ in., and repeat at each side of the panel. Draw a line 1 in. from the seam and topstitch with straight or satin stitch.

7 For the first round, take the fourth fabric and cut a strip, 2½ x 44 in. Fold in half lengthwise (wrong sides together) and press. Mark a stitching line ½ in. from the folded edge. Place this folded edge against the top stitching on the panel, cut to length, and stitch the strips across the top and bottom, then across each side, sewing on the marked line.

8 The second round of folded strips is in the third fabric. Cut a strip 2½ in. wide across the width of the fabric. Fold and press, then mark the stitching line ½ in. from the folded edge as before. Place the fold against the previous line of stitching, cut the length of the strip to fit, and stitch to the top, bottom, and sides along the marked line.

9 The third and last round does not need the extra seam allowance because the final border lies flat against the backing. From the fourth fabric cut the strips 1½ in. wide, fold in half, and press, then stitch down ½ in. from the fold, leaving ¼ in. between the stitching line and raw edges.

Below: For the wave panel, dark and light can be reversed, as seen in this sample.

FINISHING

10 From the ½ yd. piece of fabric, cut a 3 in. border. This is to be added all around the outside. Place the border fabric right sides down, first against the top and bottom, then stitch and press the strips flat against the backing. Stitch borders to the sides, again pressing the strips flat down against the backing. Trim the block to 16½ in. Using the remaining fabric from the ½ yd. piece, make up the pillow back. Insert the zipper.

11 Place the wave pillow front and back together, wrong sides out, with zipper closed. Stitch together through all layers, taking a ¼ in. seam allowance. Trim the seam and finish with a zigzag stitch. Open the zipper and turn right sides out.

Below: Pin tuck panel with first border

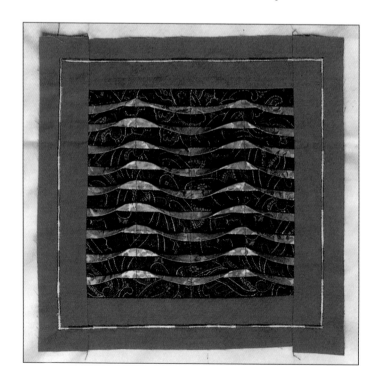

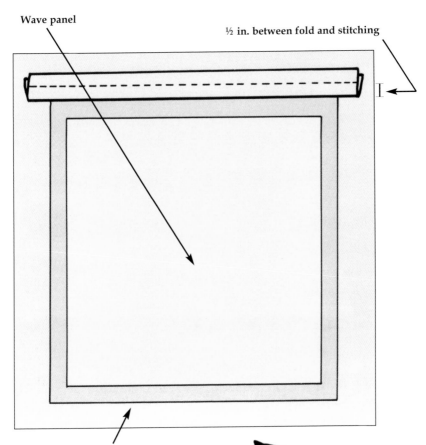

Wave panel

½ in. between fold and stitching

Line of stitching ½ in. from the seam

Above: To add the folded strips, first sew a folded strip across the top and bottom, then across each side. Place folded strip against the line of stitching on inner border and sew down ½ in. from folded edge.

The finished wave pillow

Inspiration from Artists

The work of contemporary quilt-makers is celebrated in exhibitions, books, and magazines the world over. The current revival of interest in quilt-making began in the last quarter of the twentieth century and heralded a new approach to this traditional craft. In 1971 an exhibition at the Whitney Museum of American Art in New York, "Abstract Design in American Quilts," made the groundbreaking point that quilts ought to be considered as a major influence in contemporary abstract art, and just as importantly, they were formally recognized as more than merely domestic bedcovers. Many quilt-makers embraced the new movement toward designing quilts purely as art for walls, while a new approach to the use of fabric and thread attracted artists to use the quilt as their preferred medium for expression.

There can be no doubt that the art quilt is now firmly established and is internationally recognized as making an important contribution to the world of contemporary quilt-making. In the following pages are just some examples of work from artists around the world who have chosen the quilt as their medium.

Bittersweet II

"Bittersweet II is one of a series of quilts using fall tree imagery. My recent return to tree imagery follows much abstract work using torn fabric, directly appliquéd. There is a return to tighter construction methods, such as the use of seams which protect the cut edge of the fabric. This tree imagery differs from my earlier work in its ethereal quality, created by using paint and organza fabric. I feel these trees echo my interest in both the inner and outer selves and the ensuing dialogue between the two."

Erika Carter

Natural imagery is a major influence in Erika's quilts, especially that of trees and the healing qualities of nature. She has worked through various styles of quilt-making. Here, she has abandoned earlier techniques of strip-pieced backgrounds in favor of a freer approach—that of hand-painting a background of combined cotton and silk organza, onto which floating shapes are directly hand-appliquéd. The glowing colors

Size: 69 x 51 in.

The rich shades of fall foliage in a New England woodland, as in this photograph above, are reflected in *Bittersweet II*.

of the background, pieced in broad vertical sections, form a canvas for hand-painted trees. The addition of the semiabstract leaf shapes, which float over the whole surface, add movement. The impression is one of regret for the last golden rays of sunshine that occur on fall days.

With the overall design, a composition of painted trees is superimposed onto a background of broad, vertical columns. Subtle color changes are created by hand painting, but the seams joining the columns are hard-edged, to contrast with the free drawing of the trees—silhouetted, they contrast starkly with the incandescent background.

The seams that join the background fabric are an integral part of the composition, underlining the vertical emphasis established by the trees.

ABOUT THE ARTIST

Erika Carter lives in Bellevue, Washington, with her husband and two children. She combines her sewing skills and innate sense of color to create self-expressive quilts and over the years has produced more than 200 art quilts, receiving many awards for her work. Erika is also a founding member of the Contemporary Quilt Art Association, a group dedicated to furthering the acceptance of the quilt as fine art.

Dreaming in Color

"I trained originally as a painter, and in more recent times studied patchwork and quilting, progressing from traditional techniques to using textiles as a vehicle to express my ideas. Initially these are developed from sketches, paintings, and collages in my notebooks. This provides me with color combinations and design possibilities, but often the quilts are as much about less tangible concepts like emotions and dreams. Some of my work combines unlikely influences, for instance lyrics of Bob Dylan songs with the work of artist Friedrich Hundertwasser. This quilt is one of an ongoing series inspired by the work of this painter."

Linda Kemshall

The architectural work of artist Friedrich Hundertwasser inspired a whole series of quilts, including *Dreaming in Color*.

The richly textured, abstract composition overleaf features a mixture of techniques and media. Machine appliqué, free-motion machine quilting, hand-stitched embellishment, beading, and foiling are all integrated. Materials include cotton, silk, and tiny beads. Linda first created the surface design by dyeing the basic cotton and silk fabrics. Tiny reflective beads and a combination of free-motion machine-quilting and random hand-stitching added further texture. The scattered shapes reflect the artist's internal themes, and a dreamlike quality is created by the repeated receding shapes.

The quilt is composed of four rectangles of varying sizes, each one a complete image in itself but linked by echoing shapes, some of which stray across the dividing spaces. Flashes of yellow and reflective foil enliven the somber color palette.

The shapes were bonded to the background, then machine-appliquéd using a close satin stitch in brightly colored threads.

Seeding (a form of stitching in which short, straight stitches are worked in random directions) was worked over large areas of the surface with a thick thread. This was combined with free-motion machine quilting to provide a variety of textures.

ABOUT THE ARTIST

Linda Kemshall lives and works on the Staffordshire and Shropshire borders in central England. She exhibits and lectures in Europe and North America.

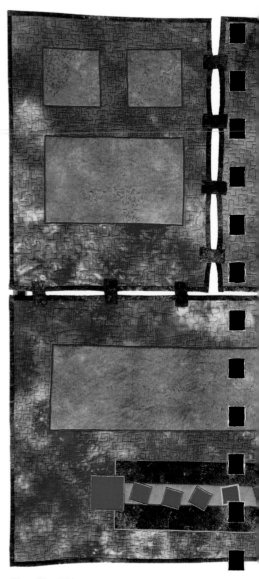

Size: 39 x 76 in.

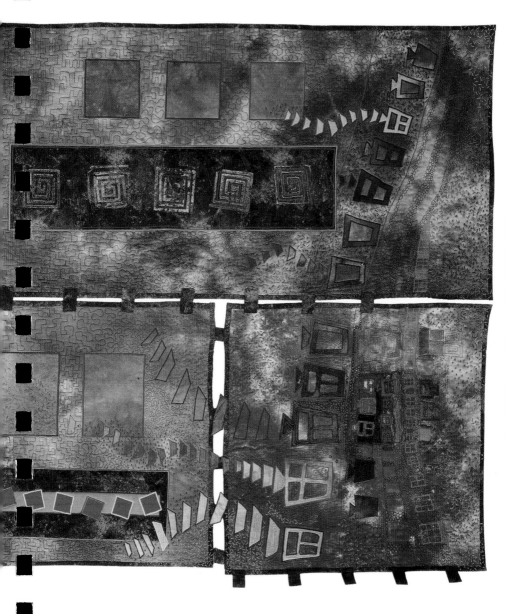

Flamboyant

"I grew up in South Africa where there was no tradition of quilt-making. I taught myself paper template (English) piecing, then after moving to Canada, I began to investigate American quilt-making techniques. I enjoy the fact that the art of quilting is evolving – quilt-makers continue to invent new techniques and break rules in the creation of unique work – and that I am part of that exciting evolution. I also cherish the fact that the art of the needle is, in essence, the voice of women, and quilting has become a powerful medium for women to tell their stories."

Valerie Hearder

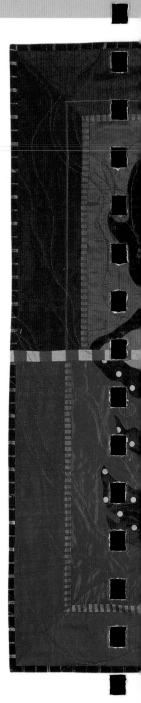

An exercise to make a design that could be repeated four times to make a spiral was the starting point for *Flamboyant*. Initially done as a woodcut print, Valerie realized it had the potential to be developed into a quilt. Striped and dotted taffeta was selected as the background for the four main blocks. The main, orange-yellow flame/flower motif has details such as veins, and flame or leaf shapes added to it. Ensuring that the borders complemented the main flower shape was a challenge; the spiral, flowing movements of the central design continue into the border via quilting. The use of taffeta gives the quilt a rich surface reflection, adding to the impact of this striking design.

Size: 51 x 51 in.

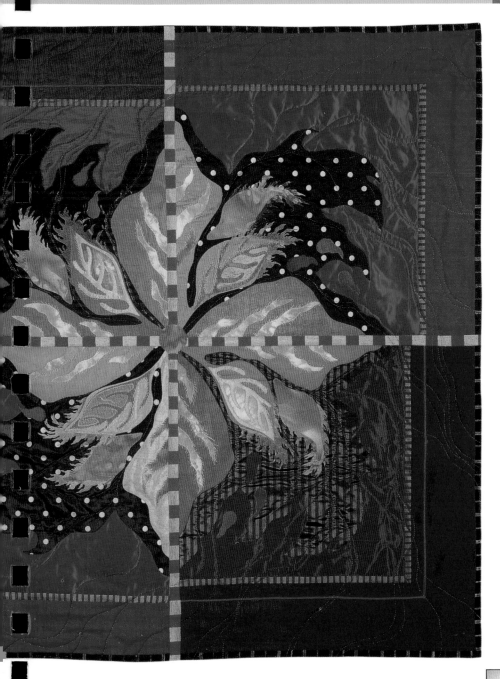

As you can see from this photograph, the essence of the flaming red and orange blossoms of the South African flamboyant tree (royal poinciana) and its likeness to fire are vividly captured in Valerie's quilt.

fabric combinations differ in opposite blocks and the small details in the central section have slight variations in their treatment.

An "aura," or fiery halo, of gold mesh was fused into place around the tips of some of the smaller leaf shapes. The main, larger shapes were simple, so Valerie added further elements, such as the hand-stitched veins, to embellish some of the edges. Free-motion quilting in variegated metallic threads echoes the main shapes in the quilt and takes them into the borders.

The central flame/flower motif in hot, vibrant colors seems to shimmer in front of the darker background colors. The narrow sashing, which divides the four sections, emphasizes the repetition and clarifies the structure of the four blocks. The dynamic design, vibrant colors, and lustrous fabrics create a quilt full of impact.

A number of techniques were combined in the making of the quilt: fusible appliqué, hand appliqué, machine piecing, machine-quilting, and hand stitching.

Although the quilt is a four-block repeat, there are variations between the blocks to add interest to the quilt. The background

ABOUT THE ARTIST

Valerie Hearder left her homeland of South Africa in 1975 and currently lives in Newfoundland, Canada. Well known for her miniature landscapes, she wrote a book on this topic, *Beyond the Horizon*. Valerie's work is found in both private and corporate collections, she teaches internationally, and her work has appeared in numerous publications.

Umbrella Thorn Tree

"I trained as a home economics teacher and have taught dressmaking, tailoring, and machine embroidery. I experimented with quilt-making in the mid-1970s but seriously started in the late 1980s. I now teach machine-quilting and machine appliqué full-time. I have always loved sewing machines and have challenged myself to do on the sewing machine what others do by hand. This piece brings back wonderful memories of a trip to South Africa in 1996."

Maurine Noble

This landscape photograph of South Africa and, in particular, memories retained in a picture taken in Shakaland, were the inspiration behind *Umbrella Thorn Tree*.

Using a collection of cotton fabrics, Maurine has created an evocative landscape. There is an element of formal simplification in the composition that increases the impact of this dramatic scene. The main foreground image of the tree is set against distant mountains. The broad border, rather than just acting as a frame, contrives to be a continuation of the picture, thanks to a clever value shift that creates a sort of transparency. As a result, the central image seems to glow, fusing color, light, and space. After drawing the design in its full size on paper, Maurine made templates for piecing. The perfectly executed narrow strips and sharp points command our admiration, but the quilt succeeds as much for its expressive qualities as for its technical virtuosity.

Here, the medium of quilt-making is used to create a textile painting. The fabrics chosen for the disparate elements—a mixture of hand-dyed cotton, commercial prints, and South African textiles—are perfect, the textured batiks working well with the large-scale abstract prints to interpret the landscape. The free-motion machine-quilting, stitched in fluid curves, unifies the separate areas of the composition and adds surface texture.

Maurine loves to machine-quilt, and her expertise is displayed beautifully in the fluid overall stitching that covers the surface of the quilt.

ABOUT THE ARTIST

Maurine Noble of Seattle, Washington, has been developing and teaching machine-quilting and machine appliqué since 1987. She has authored two books, *Machine Quilting Made Easy* and *Basic Quiltmaking Techniques for Machine Appliqué*, and coauthored *Machine Quilting with Decorative Threads*.

Size: 38½ x 32 in.

Designing Your Own Quilt

It you have worked through some of the projects in this book and experimented with different quilting skills, you may well be at the stage where you would like to design your own quilted project using your own quilting pattern. Where do you start?
If you follow a few very simple steps in developing your ideas, you'll find that you can easily work out the kind of design you want and then work through sensible ways of applying it to your chosen item. Developing your ideas step-by-step will keep you from getting bogged down with unformed ideas.

Once you're familiar with the basic techniques of quilting, you'll soon begin to see the seeds of quilting designs in almost everything around you! Architecture, carpet patterns, wrought ironwork, patterns of light on water, drapery fabrics — virtually any decorative shape can be turned into a quilting pattern of some kind. In these pages we look at the development of three very different quilting designs from the same source of inspiration. You can apply the same process of developing a design to any pattern that you think might have possibilities.

THE ROUGH IDEAS
First of all, take a large sheet of paper — or several sheets — and just sketch away very roughly, allowing the shapes themselves to

suggest patterns and combinations to you. Don't try to make the designs neat at this stage, as this will interrupt the flow of your thoughts. Put shapes together, turn them around at angles, do mirror images, use them in different sizes, overlap them, and so on (the drawings here show this process at work). Scribble notes alongside your rough designs as you get different ideas for textures, fabrics, techniques, colors, and patterns.

SELECTING DESIGN IDEAS
By this stage, you will begin to get a feel for which combinations and patterns you think will work best. Try these ideas out on fresh sheets of paper a little more neatly to see how they look in isolation and how you might use them for your quilting project.

It may be that the shape itself will suggest a particular quilted item to you. Think through which quilting technique (or techniques) will be most suitable and what threads and colors you feel would work best.

FINISHED DESIGN
Draw your design neatly to the required size. At this stage, measure lines and curves carefully and make sure that all the shapes of the pattern are consistent. Try out different fabrics and threads against the pattern to see what works best. You may want to work a small trial piece in your chosen materials to check that the texture and balance are right. Once you are completely happy, transfer the design to your chosen fabric and start quilting!

WORKING THROUGH A DESIGN
Every time you have an idea for a quilting project, jot it down somewhere; otherwise you'll forget it. You may find it helpful to keep a special notebook or file specifically for this purpose. You don't need to draw it neatly; just make a quick sketch or scribble down written ideas, such as "Try something based on the patterns of Indian rugs." Then, when you're in a creative mood, you can pull out your ideas and select which ones you wish to turn into finished designs.

Here you can see how I worked through the design process for a quilt — right from the very first scribbles of inspiration to the finished piece.

THE FIRST IDEA
When I go on vacation, I take a notebook with me for writing down quilting and embroidery ideas, but most of the time I just scribble them on the back of old photocopies and put them in a file

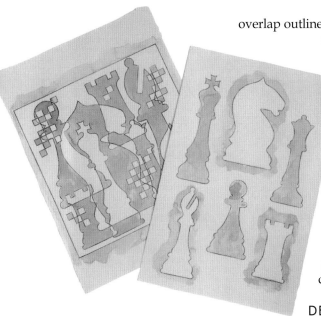

overlap outlines of chess pieces of different sizes, building in an interchange of black and white. When I tried to draw even a rough scribble, I realized how ignorant I was of just what the pieces looked like, so I made a note to myself to research the different shapes.

The final design for the chess quilt, incorporating the chess pieces in different sizes.

alongside interesting photographs, cards, and textures torn from magazines and brochures. This quilt began as one of those scribbles.

I am utterly uninterested in the game of chess, but I have always been fascinated by the shapes of chess pieces and the wonderful contrasts offered by the constantly changing arrangements of black and white as the pieces move across the board. It suddenly occurred to me one evening what a striking design it would make to

DETERMINING THE SHAPES

I went to the library and looked at books about playing chess and about collecting chess sets. I made photocopies of many interesting sets for later reference.

DECIDING ON THE DESIGN ELEMENTS

Reluctantly, I had to abandon less conventional shapes, including some of the more abstract modern ones, as I felt it was important for the shapes to be instantly recognizable as chess pieces. These line drawings show the final shapes I decided on for the pieces; they are a hybrid of several standard chess set designs.

THE DESIGN ITSELF

I wanted the quilt to be square—to echo the shape of the chessboard itself—so I drew a large square on paper and began sketching in the shapes in different sizes, erasing and redrawing as the design took shape.

My aim was to end up with a good contrast of sizes among the shapes, as I felt that otherwise they would tend to blur into each other. I also wanted to introduce several random areas of checkering to emphasize the chess theme and to provide visual interest. First of all, I made these of varying-sized squares, as I had done with the pieces themselves. This proved too distracting, so I changed them so that the checkers were all the same size. The drawing at left shows the final design I came up with, shaded roughly to indicate the areas of black and white.

THE QUILT ITSELF

I enlarged the design in sections on a photocopier, since I liked the flow of the lines I had come up with and didn't want to lose them by enlarging the design freehand.

When I had traced the design onto fabric, I painted it in with black fabric paint.

I considered appliquéing the black areas, but I wanted to quilt them with a thin line of machine stitching around the shapes, so felt that it was better not to have raw edges.

I layered the finished design with fairly thick batting and white backing fabric, then bound the edges with the backing fabric to complete it. It's come a long way since that first experimental scribble. . . .

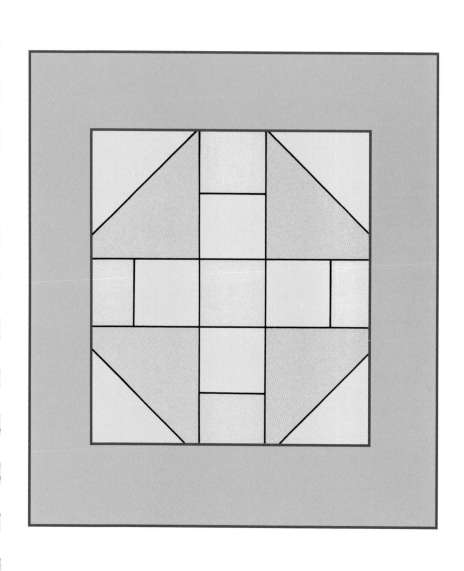

Classic pillow cover A

Classic pillow cover B

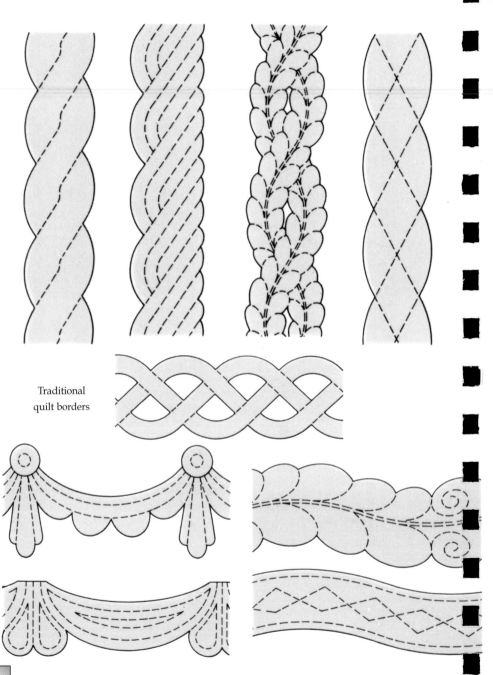

Traditional
quilt borders

Traditional motifs of circles, flowers, leaves, fans, and shells

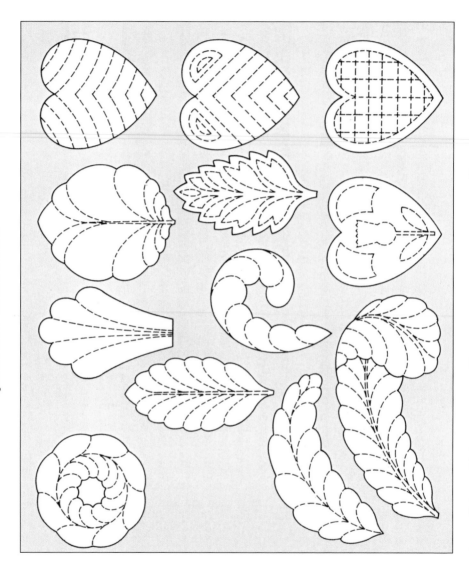

Traditional motifs of flowers, leaves, and hearts

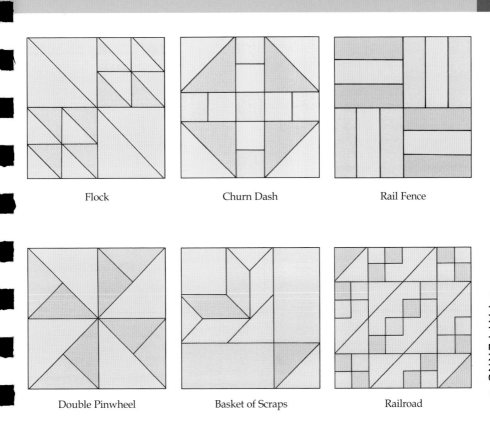

Flock

Churn Dash

Rail Fence

Double Pinwheel

Basket of Scraps

Railroad

This page shows a selection of traditional American blocks in color to show how the combinations can be used.

The following pages show a selection of block designs that range from easy (**E** – squares and triangles) to moderately easy (**ME** – rhomboid) to difficult (**D** – for the more experienced patchworker).

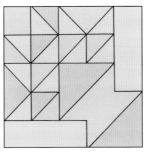

Fruit Basket

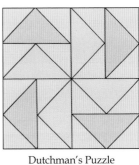

Dutchman's Puzzle

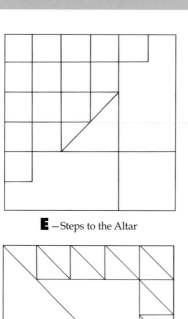

E —Steps to the Altar

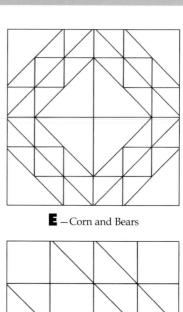

E —Corn and Bears

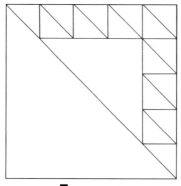

E —Sawtooth

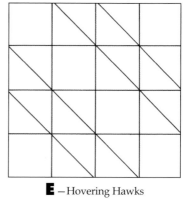

E —Hovering Hawks

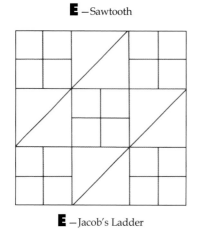

E —Jacob's Ladder

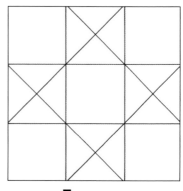

E —Ohio Star

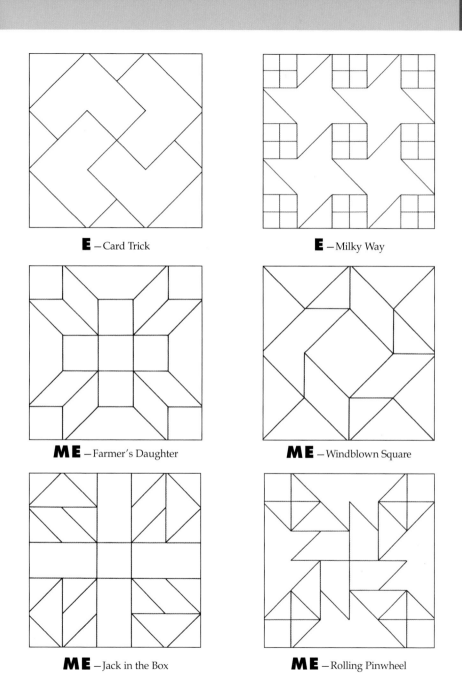

E – Card Trick

E – Milky Way

ME – Farmer's Daughter

ME – Windblown Square

ME – Jack in the Box

ME – Rolling Pinwheel

ME – Clay's Choice

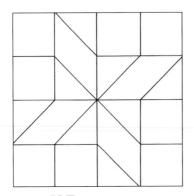

ME – Pieced Star

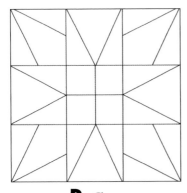

D – Claws

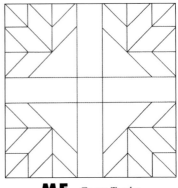

ME – Arrowheads

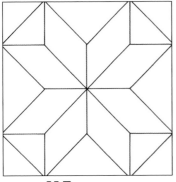

ME – Goose Tracks

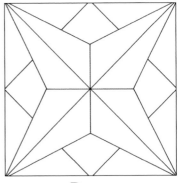

D – Star

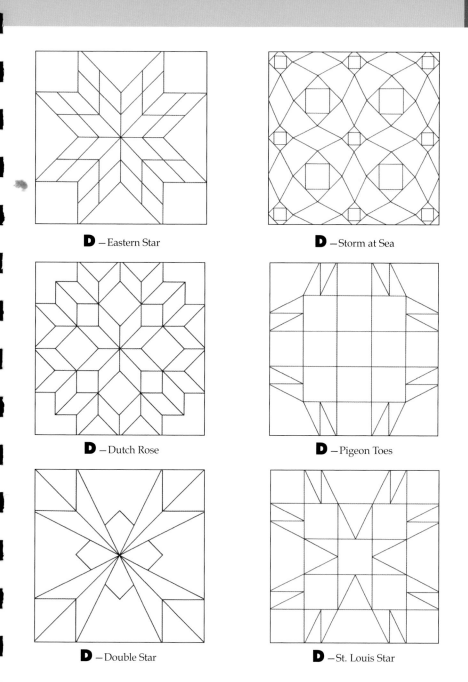

D – Eastern Star

D – Storm at Sea

D – Dutch Rose

D – Pigeon Toes

D – Double Star

D – St. Louis Star

Glossary

Accent stitch An embroidery stitch that is chiefly used to provide a splash of color or texture.

Appliqué Shapes of different fabrics are placed on the ground fabric to form a design and secured by tiny stitches that are hardly seen, or by a decorative embroidery stitch.

Awl A sharp-pointed instrument used for making holes in fabric.

Backing The piece of fabric used on the underside of a quilt.

Baste or **tack** Temporary stitches to hold fabric in place until smaller, more secure stitching is done.

Batting or **wadding** The insulating filler in a quilt.

Bias Any slanting or oblique line in relation to the warp and weft threads of a fabric. The true bias is formed when the selvage is folded at a right angle across the fabric parallel to the weft and runs exactly forty-five degrees to the straight grain.

Binding A strip of fabric stitched around the outer edges of the work, neatening and enclosing raw edges.

Block The design unit on which American patchwork is based.

Bodkin A long, blunt-edged needle with a large eye, used for threading tape, cord, or elastic through a channel or casing.

Border stitch A wide embroidery stitch that is always used in a straight line and makes a very attractive border. Multiple rows can be worked to make a more complex decorative border.

Couching A technique in which a thick thread or group of threads is attached to the ground fabric by means of a finer thread. It is particularly suitable for textured and metallic threads that cannot be stitched directly into the fabric.

Dressing A stiffening agent of starch, gum, kaolin (china clay), or size found in new fabrics. Sometimes hides poor-quality fabric but can also be an integral part of the fabric, as in glazed chintz.

Edging stitch An embroidery stitch used to finish a raw edge to prevent the fabric from fraying, or to decorate a plain hemmed edge.

Encroaching stitches A term used to describe the overlap of one row of stitching with the preceding row.

Even-weave fabric A fabric with warp and weft threads of identical thicknesses that provide the same number of threads over a given area, enabling the threads to be counted to keep the stitching even.

Fabric grain The line of the warp thread in a piece of fabric.

Frame A square or rectangular wooden frame used to keep fabric taut during stitching.

Gauge The number of threads that can be stitched in 1 in. of canvas. Also the number of threads or woven blocks that can be stitched in 1 in. of even-weave fabric.

Grain The line of the warp in woven fabric. Straight grain runs parallel to the selvage and has the least amount of stretch. Cross grain runs from selvage to selvage and has the least amount of stretch. Bias grain cuts across the fabric diagonally and has the most stretch. Cutting horizontally along the weft is known as cutting across (or against) the grain.

Matte embroidery cotton A tightly twisted, five-ply thread with a matte finish, always used as a single thread.

Miter The diagonal line formed at forty-five degrees to the edges of fabric joined to form a ninety-degree angle.

Motif stitch An embroidery stitch that is worked individually, with each stitch making a distinctive shape.

Patchwork The process of making a large piece of fabric from smaller ones.

Pearl cotton A twisted, two-ply thread with a lustrous sheen. It cannot be divided into separate strands but it is available in three different weights.

Piecing The sewing together of small pieces of fabric to form a larger whole piece.

Pin tucks A series of very narrow tucks stitched on the right side of the fabric and used as decoration.

Quilt An embroidery made from three layers of fabric, consisting of the top (often decorative patchwork), the insulating filler, and the backing.

Quilting Running stitches that hold the three layers of the quilt together. These can be done by hand or machine.

Raw edge The unfinished edge of a fabric.

Scrim Fine, open-weave canvas of a light brown color, originally made from low-grade linen but may be cotton or a mixture of other fibers.

Selvage The finished edges of a piece of fabric running the length of the fabric along either side.

Shadow embroidery A type of embroidery done on a semitransparent fabric.

Stranded floss A loosely twisted, slightly shiny, six-strand cotton thread. For fine embroidery, the threads can be separated and used in twos or threes.

Stranded silk A pure silk similar to stranded floss but with a more lustrous finish.

Tapestry needle A long, thick needle with a blunt tip and a large eye.

Template The pattern from which patchwork shapes are cut. They are made of stiff material such as cardboard, plastic, or metal.

Vanishing muslin Stiffened, treated muslin used as a backing or support for some hand and machine embroidery. The stitching is done through both layers and the surplus muslin vanishes when pressed with a warm iron.

Warp The threads in a woven fabric that run lengthwise on the weaving loom.

Waxed thread A thread that has been strengthened by rubbing it against a block of beeswax.

Weft The threads running across the width of woven fabric that are interwoven with the warp threads.

Index

PAGE NUMBERS IN ITALICS REFER TO ILLUSTRATIONS AND CAPTIONS.

A

abrasive paper 14
acetate 14
appliqué 63–5
artist's quilted work
  192–203, *192–6,*
  199–203

B

baby's coverlet 113–16,
  113–16
baby's jacket 108–12,
  108–9, 111–12
bias binding 31
Bittersweet II 193
bright rug 147–52,
  147–9, 151–2

C

card trick shoulder bag
  180–3, *181–3*
cardboard 14
Chinese headboard
  128–135, *128–33, 135*
Christmas tree 164–8,
  164, 166–8
classic pillow covers
  78–81, *78–81*
clutch purse 102–7, *102,*
  105–7
contour quilting 38–41,
  38–41

corded quilting 57–9,
  57–9
cording 33

D

designing your own
  quilt 205–6
  working through a
  design 207–8
Dreaming in Color 195

E

equipment 11
  cutting 17
  general drawing
  equipment 12–15, *12,*
  15
  general sewing
  equipment 16–19,
  17–19

F

Flamboyant 198
frames 16

G

greeting cards 87–91, *87,*
  89, 91

I

inspiration from artists
  191

Bittersweet II — Erika
  Carter 193
Dreaming in Color —
  Linda Kemshall 195
Flamboyant — Valerie
  Hearder 198
Umbrella Thorn Tree —
  Maurine Noble 201
irons 18

L

lace, eyelet lace, and
  ribbon 32

M

materials 20–1, *20,*
  22–24
mirror frame 97–101,
  97, 99, 101

N

nautilus tea cozy 75–7,
  75–7
needles 16
nightgown case 141–6,
  141–6

P

paper 14
patchwork 67–71
  American block 67
  blocks 67

patterns 209
  American blocks, color 215
  American blocks, difficult 219
  American blocks, easy 216
  American blocks, easy/moderately easy 217
  American blocks, moderately easy/difficult 218
  classic pillow cover 210–11
  quilted borders 212
  quilted motifs 213–14
pencil or sewing kit case 175–9, *175–9*
pins 16
place mats 82–6, *82–6*
plain hems 33
projects
  baby's coverlet 113–16, *113–16*
  baby's jacket 108–112, *108–9, 111–12*
  bright rug 147–152, *147–9, 151–2*
  card trick shoulder bag 180–3, *180, 182–3*
  Chinese headboard 128–135, *128–133, 135*
  Christmas tree 165–8, *166–8*
  classic pillow covers 78–81, *78–81*
  clutch purse 102–7, *102, 105–7*

greeting cards 87–91, *87, 88, 91*
mirror frame 97–101, *97, 101*
nautilus tea cozy 74–7, *74–7*
nightgown case 141–6, *141–6*
pencil or sewing kit case 175–9, *175–9*
place mats 82–6, *82–6*
quilted play mat 153–7, *153–7*
rainbow cushion 122–7, *122, 124–7*
rose picture 117–121, *117–121*
spring wall hanging 136–140, *136–140*
stained glass quilt 158–163, *158–9, 161–3*
striped jerkin *169–174, 169, 171–4*
water lily curtain 92–6, *92, 95–6*
wave pillow 184–9, *184, 186–9*

Q

quilt filler 21
quilted play mat 153–7, *153–7*
quilting
  and appliqué 63–6, *64–6*
  contour 38–41, *38–41*
  corded 57–9, *57–9*
  fabrics 20

and patchwork 67–71, *68–71*
random 46–9, *46–9*
Sashiko 60–2, *61–2*
shadow 42–5, *42–5*
techniques 25
tied 50–3, *50–3*
traditional 34–7, *34–7*
trapunto 54–6, *54–6*

R

rainbow cushion 122–27, *122, 124, 126–7*
random quilting 46–9
rose picture 117–121, *117–21*
rotary cutter 17
ruffles 31

S

Sashiko quilting 60–2
sewing machines 18
shadow quilting 42–5
spring wall hanging 136–140, *136–140*
stained glass quilt 158–163, *158–9, 161–3*
stitches
  by hand 26–7, *26–7*
  hand-quilting 26
    backstitch 26
    chain stitch 26
    running 26
  hand stitches 27
    blanket 27
    couching 27
    fly 27
    quilting 28
  by machine 28–9, *28–9*

machine-quilting 28
  satin 29
  straight 29
  zigzag 29
striped jerkin 169–74,
  169, 171–4

T

tape measure 19
techniques
  finishing 30–33, *30–33*

templates 15, 67
threads
  for hand-quilting 19
  for machine sewing 19
tied quilting 50–53
traditional quilting 34–7
trapunto quilting 54–6

U

Umbrella Thorn Tree 201
unpicker 19

W

water lily curtain 92–6,
  92, 95–6
wave pillow 184–9, *184,*
  186–9
wax 19

Picture Credits
&
Acknowledgments

The material in this book previously appeared in:

The Complete Quilting Course, by Gail Lawther

How to Create Beautiful Quilts, by Katherine Guerrier

Quilting Masterclass, by Katherine Guerrier

The Quilting Patchwork & Applique Project Book, by Dorothea Hall

The Quilting and Patchwork Project Book, by Katherine Guerrier

Quilts, by Mary Clare Clark